PAGANISM

IN THE

PAPAL CHURCH

BY

W. J. WILKINS

LATE OF CALCUTTA

Author of " Hindu Mythology," " Modern Hinduism," etc.

This book is now published by

Messrs. George Allen & Company, Ltd.

RUSKIN HOUSE,

44 & 45, RATHBONE PLACE,

OXFORD STREET, LONDON, W.

to whom all orders should be sent.

APRIL, 1911.

Preface.

THE striking resemblance between the religious practices of Hinduism and those of the Roman Catholic Church cannot fail to be noticed by those familiar with the two systems. Intelligent Hindus affirm that there is little to distinguish them. On one occasion, after addressing a Hindu audience, one of my hearers said that only a little time before, he entered a church and saw a vessel of holy water which was used for washing away sin, an image of a goddess before which the people were bowing in worship, and people confessing to a priest, hoping to obtain pardon for their sins. He asked me wherein all this differed from bathing in the Ganges, worshipping the goddess Durgā, and seeking salvation from a guru or confessor. I had to admit that in principle there was little difference between the heathen and

the Christian practice. In course of time
other ceremonies common to the two
systems were noticed, and the present
work is the result. It has been written in
the hope that some who read it may see
that in departing from the simplicity of
scriptural practice they are moving towards
the old paganism which the Church only
partially overcame.

W. J. WILKINS.

CONTENTS

INDEX.

CHAPTER I

INTRODUCTORY REMARKS

IN these days, when a determined effort is made to undo the work of the Reformation and to lead back the people to the faith and practice of mediæval times, it is our duty to examine the character of that ideal age. If our fathers were guilty in separating themselves from the Church of Rome, which claims to be "the one true Church," we must be equally guilty in continuing separate from her communion. But if they were right in denouncing the anti-Christian teaching and practices which that Church authoritatively taught, we should be guilty if we did not oppose it. For, since the Reformation, if there has been any change in Rome's doctrines it has been in a still farther departure from the simplicity of the gospel.

A careful examination of the ideal age of the Church, protesting against which has been de-

I

scribed as "a huge mistake" will show that it was not original where it differed from the faith of apostolic times. It had come to be what it was, not by a better understanding of the scriptures, and by a true developement of what was common in the early days of the Church. Without doubt it was a return to what was universal in the Roman world before Christianity became the religion of the Empire. If the original of much of its teaching and ceremony be sought it will be found in the paganism which to outward appearance it had supplanted. The conversion of the nations of Europe was superficial rather than radical. Heathenism was suppressed by imperial commands. Princes were baptized and their ignorant subjects followed their example; but unfortunately there was little opportunity of systematic instruction in Christian truth. The result was that most of the converts retained their old faiths; and the leaders of the Church made the way from heathenism to Christianity easy, by arranging their worship so as to make it scarcely distinguishable from that with which the people were familiar.

"The ruin of paganism, in the age of

Theodosius, is, perhaps, the only example of the total extirpation of any ancient and popular superstition. The imperial laws which prohibited the sacrifices and ceremonies of paganism were rigidly executed and every hour contributed to destroy a religion, which was supported by custom rather than by argument. The generation which arose in the world after the promulgation of the imperial laws [forbidding the old idolatry] was attracted within the pale of the Catholic Church; and so rapid, yet so gentle, was the fall of paganism, that only twenty-eight years after the death of Theodosius, the faint and minute vestiges were no longer visible to the eye of the legislator."[1] But, though the old religion had nominally disappeared, in the same chapter the historian gives a picture of what was going on in the Christian Church, and affirms that if a saint of a previous century had risen from the dead and witnessed the ceremonies he would have been indignant at the heathen practices then common.

Facts abundantly confirm the historian's words. Some of the beautiful temples of the old gods

[1] *Decline and Fall of the Roman Empire* chap. xxviii.

were ruthlessly destroyed by zealous partisans; but others, without much change, were converted into churches. Some of the universally honoured images were broken to pieces; others were retained as representatives of the Virgin Mary or some great Saint. Popes sometimes condemned this practice, but the superstitions of ignorant people were too strong to be resisted. One of our own Saxon kings insisted on having an altar on which sacrifices were offered to the devil in the same building in which God was worshipped. The vessel of holy water, which of old had stood at the entrance of the temples, in which the worshippers could wash away ceremonial defilement, remained in its place to be used by Christians in a similar manner. Certain days sacred to some of the lesser gods of paganism, became associated with Christian Saints, and similar ceremonies were performed at their festivals. By the introduction of the confessional, the priests, professing to have the power to absolve or condemn, secured a firm hold upon the people, just as their predecessors had who initiated members into the mysteries of heathen deities. Shrines, where special boons could be obtained, soon became common, and marvellous stories were circulated to induce pilgrims to visit them. The doctrine of purgatory, a place where departed spirits were held in misery until their surviving friends secured their release by costly ceremonies, was in perfect harmony with what had been taught in pagan times. In fact there was scarcely a superstition or practice of the old system, that did not sooner or later find its way into the Christian Church.

The great evils which the Reformation sought to eradicate were not introduced in the dimensions they had by that time attained. At first the departure from primitive practice was slight and apparently harmless. In innocence and good faith some leader took a single step on a diverging road, scarcely noticing the divergence. Others, endowed with clearer vision and truer insight, saw, deplored, and condemned the innovations. Unfortunately their warnings were unheeded. And, in the course of centuries, the path which at first seemed almost parallel to that by which the Master walked, was seen to lead away from the desired goal. It cannot therefore be too clearly stated that for Protestants to go back to the faiths and practices of the Mediæval Church, is a return, not to a purer, but to a debased form of the Christian religion ; to the paganism of Rome rather than to the teaching of Jesus Christ and His apostles.   It is the object of this book to show how the old heathenism of Rome was quietly adopted and adapted by the leaders of the Christian Church.

In tracing the corruptions of the Church to the heathenism it nominally overcame, one appears to be an enemy attacking his brethren. But this is not the case. / It is not the charge of an opponent more than the boast of the leaders of the Roman Catholic Church that they adopted much of the heathenism they were professedly attempting to overthrow./ They acknowledge and glory in the fact.   In their judgment it is a modern illustration of spoiling the Egyptians. Unfortunately, by this process the Church was paganised, rather than the nations Christianized. As a specimen of the way in which authorities in the Roman Catholic Church have written on this subject, the following may be given. " If we closely investigate the subject we shall perceive that many institutions of our religion have been taken and translated from Egyptian and heathen ceremonies.   Of this kind are tunics and surplices, the crowns made by our priests, their bowings around the altar, sacrificial pomp, the music of the temple, adorations, prayers and supplications, processions and litanies. These and many other things which the folly and superstitious ignorance of the heathen refer to their gods and deified men, our priests adopt in our mysteries, and refer to the one sole God, Jesus Christ."[1] " In order to win the Pagans to Christ, instead of Pagan watchings and commemorations of their gods, the Christians rejoiced in vigils and anniversaries of their martyrs ; and, to show that they had regard to the public prosperity, in place of those feasts in which the heathen were wont to supplicate the gods for the welfare of their country, they introduced rogations, litanies and processions made with naked feet, invoking Christ instead of Jupiter ; and this is the reason why our fêtes and ceremonies have generally a pagan origin."[2] In another passage Picart declares that " this mode of acting was not intended to paganize, but wisely ? to countermine paganism, and, as a compromise, to parry the reproaches that the

[1] Du Choul, quoted in *Rome Pagan and Papal*, p. 10.

[2] Picart in do., p. 26

Pagans made against the Christians." In his instructions to his missionaries in the sixth century, proving conclusively that by that time the evil was well nigh done, and that familiarity with Pagan practices had made Christian teachers tolerant of them, Pope Gregory told them to meet the heathen half-way, and thus make their conversion easy. Hobart Seymour, in his "Pilgrimage to Rome," says : " In every land Romanists are usually indignant when it is said that their ceremonies were originally heathen. In Italy, on the other hand, that origin is claimed for them, as a proof of the wisdom of a Church which has converted a heathen people, and their heathen customs, into a Christian people, and Christian ceremonies." With statements such as these before us, from accredited teachers of the Roman Church, we may indicate the origin of what we consider worthy of condemnation without violating the law of charity.

The history of the Church shows conclusively that the practice of adopting pagan customs that are not in complete harmony with the teaching of its Head, however good the intention, has been fruitful of the gravest evil. The learned few may be able to separate them from their former connexion, the ignorant many cannot. However helpful a practice may seem to be, if it is opposed to the precepts of our divine Master it should be avoided. Possibly if those who innocently introduced innovations could see to what their conduct led they would cry out loudly in condemnation of them. When Satan offered to the Saviour the dominion of the world on condition that He would fall down and worship him, the answer was " Get thee behind me, Satan." How different would have been the history of the Church if His followers had always acted in a similar spirit.

Many in the Roman Catholic Church are better than their creed. Though we differ from them on many most important matters, we agree on more. Take up any good collection of hymns, and it will be seen how many of the choicest compositions have been written by members of that Church. There is nothing to indicate their theological position. It is the measure of truth in its teaching that has saved it, for some of its errors are great indeed.

In the religious history of Japan we find a striking analogy to what occurred in Europe

When Buddhist missionaries reached Japan they found the people devoted to an elaborate system of Nature worship, the sun being the Supreme. The missionaries wishing to conciliate the people assured them that the Buddha whom they preached and the sun and other deities were the same. They told them to add Buddha to their other objects of worship, and perform additional rites which they would teach, and their happiness would be assured. In time the work of their new teachers was successful, and the people, influenced by their rulers, openly accepted the Buddhist faith. But what is the result? The two systems are in force; and the professed followers of Gautama Buddha, who, concerning the existence of God, was a consistent agnostic, continue to worship the gods of their fathers. The temples of the two religions are often side by side, and the people readily perform the ceremonies of both, though in many respects they are diametrically opposed.

In the following chapters, illustrations will be given of pagan beliefs and practices still common in the Christian Church.

CHAPTER II

AUTHORITY IN FAITH AND PRACTICE

WHERE there is the belief in a revelation of God, the book in which it is contained, one would imagine, would be universally accepted as the authoritative standard in all matters of which it treats; and that every proper means would be employed to bring it within reach of, and make it intelligible to the people. By the Protestant it is accepted as an axiom that the Bible, given by divine inspiration, ought to be read by all, and its lessons implicitly obeyed. But this doctrine is not regarded as axiomatic by the Romanist. He says that the Church is to define the doctrine, and regulate the practice. In a letter written from the Vatican by Mgr. Talbot to the late Cardinal Manning this is very tersely put. "What is the province of the laity? To hunt, to shoot, to entertain. These matters they understand; but to meddle with ecclesias-

tical matters they have no right at all."[1]   It is
the work of the Church, i.e., the Priests, with the
Pope as the head, to read and interpret the
Word of God ; to add to, to desregard its
plainest teaching : it is the duty of those outside
the priesthood to accept their statements and
leave the Bible alone. A privileged class has
usurped and retained possession of one of the
most blessed privileges of the Christian.

Before considering at length the teaching of
the Church of Rome on this important question
it will be interesting to notice a very striking
analogy in modern Hinduism.   Many pagan
systems have a similar rule.

Amongst the many ways of salvation which
Hinduism provides, there is one vastly superior
to the rest, called the way of knowledge.   Other
ways lead to heaven, a place where there is a
temporary state of happiness, this to the supreme
good, absorption into the divine. This superior
way is through the knowledge of the Vedas, the
oldest, and most highly valued of their many
inspired books. These books are " reserved " for
the members of the highest caste, and it is

[1] *Life of Cardinal Manning*, ii. 318.

affirmed to be a deadly sin for one of this privileged class to read them to, or for one of the lower caste to hear them. This knowledge is said to confer such power upon its possessors that even the gods are obliged to do their bidding. If therefore the non-privileged classes desire a boon it is natural that they should seek the powerful intercession of their more favoured brethren, and be ready to pay a good price to secure it.

But as the common people wanted inspired books, others are specially prepared for them. These have been written with a purpose. In the older, and carefully " reserved " works, the caste distinctions declared to be of divine appointment, have no place. In those earlier days, the heads of families are instructed to offer gifts and sacrifices. No mention is made of a privileged class of priests, possessing the exclusive right of approaching the gods. These books, now carefully guarded from the common people, were the property of all. In the course of centuries great changes in the life of the people gradually came about. The privilege of directly approaching the gods was withdrawn from the low caste people and made the function of the priestly caste. As these changes are opposed to the spirit and letter of the older books, a text was inserted in them prohibiting their use to any but the members of the highest caste. And in the more modern books which have been provided for the people generally, marvellous stories are found to lead the people to pay honour to the Brahmans, only, if at all, inferior to that which is given to the gods. To put this Hindu practice into the terms of Christianity; the Brahmans have "reserved" the Vedas as unsuitable for the masses, pleading divine sanction for them; and have prepared a series of works better suited to meet their wants. On comparing the two classes of literature it is evident that this has been done to extract the homage of those who have been defrauded, and to make them believe that those who have defrauded them can exert peculiar influence over their deities. Were the older books read by the people generally it would be impossible to harmonize recent practice with ancient precept.

In principle, there is little difference between Hinduism and Roman Catholicism in this important matter. Where the Romish Church is free to carry out her plans, uninfluenced by

an enlightened public opinion, the Bible is a
sealed book ; and in communities where there
is no distinct order forbidding its use, no effort
is made to put it within reach of her members.
Where it has been translated into the common
language, the priests have rather discouraged
than encouraged their people to read it.
Ximenes, Prime Minister of Spain, in the reign
of Ferdinand and Isabella expressed the common
faith of his order.   When the Moors were
conquered, and the choice was offered them of
embracing Christianity, or suffering death or
banishment, a considerable number offered themselves for baptism.   A proposal was made that
as Arabic was the only language which they
could read, a copy of the New Testament should
be given to each in that tongue in order that
they might learn something of Christian
doctrine.   To this he objected that it was
" casting pearls before swine," to give the Scriptures to those who were so recently converted.
Nor would he consent for the Spaniards born in
Christian homes to have them in their own
language.   " Catechisms, solid and simple ex-
planations of Christian doctrine, and other
writings calculated to enlighten the minds of the

people he was willing to have circulated. The word of God should be wrapped in discreet mysteries from the vulgar, who feel little reverence for what is plain and obvious. The Scriptures should be confined to the three ancient languages (Hebrew, Greek, and Latin) which God with mystic import permitted to be inscribed over the head of His crucified Son ; and the vernacular should be reserved for such devotional and moral treatises as holy men indite in order to quicken the soul, and turn it from the pursuit of worldly vanities to heavenly contemplation." [1] A Spanish Archbishop, when charging his clergy was still more explicit. He instructed them to be most careful to keep the Bible, when translated into a language they could understand, out of the hands of their flocks or it would be difficult to lead them to understand the reason of much that the Church taught and commanded. We in England owe to Wycliffe a debt of gratitude that we have the word of God in our own tongue, and also freedom to read it. But how was his work regarded by his Church ? His antagonist—Knighton—thus

[1] *Memories of Spanish Reformers.* p ,32.

writes,—"Christ delivered His gospel to the
clergy and doctors of the Chnrch, that they
might administer to the laity and the weaker
persons, according to the state of the times, and
the wants of men. But this Master John
Wycliffe translated it out of Latin into the
tongue Anglican—not Angelic. Thus it became
of itself vulgar, more open to the laity, and to
women who could read, than it usually is to the
clergy, even the most learned and intelligent.
In this way the gospel-pearl is cast abroad and
trodden under foot of swine; and that which
was before precious both to clergy and to laity,
is rendered, as it were, the common jest of both."
For this grand work of giving us the Bible in
our common tongue Wycliffe was regarded by
the professed servants of our Lord and exclusive
teachers of His truth, as " the Devil's instrument,
and the Church's enemy." And though whilst he
lived he was protected from the hatred of his
enemies, thirteen years after his death, by order
of the Pope, his body was exhumed, his bones
burnt, and the ashes thrown into the river Swift,
which flowed beside his rectory at Lutterworth.

The authorized teaching of Rome on this, as
on other questions, is found in the creed of Pope

2

Pius IV.; a creed that was based upon the decisions of the Council of Trent. Owing to the circulation of what was regarded as heretical doctrine, this Council was called to define the Church's teaching. And in reference to authority in matters of doctrine, this is Rome's utterance. "Art. I. I most firmly admit and embrace the Apostolical and Ecclesiastical traditions, and all other observations and constitutions of the same Church. Art. II. I do admit the Holy Scriptures in the same sense that Holy Mother Church hath held and doth hold; whose business it is to judge of the true sense and interpretation of them. Nor will I ever receive or interpret them except according to the unanimous consent of the Fathers." In these two articles we have the position of the members of the Roman Catholic Church definitely and authoritatively determined; they have to accept the teaching which has found its way into the Church by tradition, in addition to, and of equal authority with the Bible; and they have to accept the interpretations of the Bible which the Church, i.e. the clergy, have given. It is these articles and the canons of which they are the expression which have led to the practical withdrawal of the Bible from the people.

Before this Council was called, and whilst its meetings were being held, there were pious priests and learned bishops who urged their flocks to a careful study of the Word of God. But the discussions occasioned by Luther's attack on the Papacy led people to urge the Pope to call a general council in which the questions in dispute could be settled. There were some who earnestly hoped that much needed reforms might thus be effected. When the Council assembled, unfortunately, the party of progress failed to carry out their wishes; the majority voted for the articles as they stand. On this question of authority in doctrine the more astute saw that it was dangerous to place the New Testament, with the right to read and interpret it, in the hands of the common people. So first comes the article in which faith is expressed in the immense body of traditions which have come down from past centuries; and then the statement that the Scriptures shall be accepted only in the sense in which the Church has ever held them, and interpreted only in accordance with the unanimous consent of the Fathers.

If ever an ocean was compressed into a teacup it is in the first article of Pope Pius' creed. In a short sentence acceptance is made of an immense amount of doctrine which in the longest life one would not be able even to read. According to Cardinal Manning, the four terms apostolic and ecclesiastical traditions, and observations and constitutions of the Church, "embrace every word which the Popes have uttered in every age in the matter of doctrine, rite or preccpt, whether in brief, bull, letter, encyclical, or any other of the many forms which the curialism of Rome has invented for the promulgation of her 'ukases.' These of course are supplemented, or rather preceded by the laws of the Councils, general and provincial ; by the decisions of various congregations, and by the exactions of a daily and most minute legislation, which may at any moment multiply them or abrogate them—a mass of enactments exceeding immeasurably the 'Statutes as large' with all the reports of judges and books of precedents in our own complicated system of laws. What this really means may be partially realised when it is known that the decrees of Councils fill fifty folio volumes ; the Bulls extend to over sixty similar books, whereas the published decisions of the Congregation for the interpretation of the Council of Trent and of Rites exceed both together in number and perplexity." [1]

In view of this, one has some sympathy with a story told in a pre-reformation book written for the direction of the sick and dying, to illustrate the utility of accepting the creed of the Church wholesale. "The devil," it is said, "interrogated a dying man on his faith in these words, 'What do you believe?' to which he replied. 'I believe all that the Roman Church believes.' Whereupon the interrogator rejoined, 'But what does the Roman Church believe?' to which the dying man very prudently replied, 'all that I believe myself.'" [2]

It must not be imagined that this article was accepted without protest. Many emphatically denied that the traditions of men were of equal authority with the word of God. "There is a a vast difference between scripture and tradition. For the Holy Scripture is altogether indelible, whereas many of the apostolic traditions are

[1] *Romanism*, by Rev. R. C. Jenkins, M. A. p. 56

[2] *Ibid*, p. 54.

variable, and can be changed or taken away according to the will of the Church."[1] Whilst another boldly declared that it was vain to trust in traditions when they possessed a full gospel in a written form.

When the claim is made for the authority of tradition, equal to that of the Scriptures, what is really meant is this :—that the Holy Spirit who inspired holy men to write the Scriptures, also inspired others to interpret them. But an examination of these " inspired " interpreters show them to have been at variance on almost every question. So that one may be quoted as worthy of acceptance in some cases, and unworthy in others. At the present time, the Pope professes to speak with an infallible voice to determine what the divine tradition is. As Protestants we have the Bible, containing God's revelation, and the Holy Spirit promised to every humble seeker after truth; the Romanist adds the traditions of men, with the Pope as interpreter. But when it is seen that in many cases these traditions are opposed to the inspired Word of God, we claim the right to reject them in

[1] Bishop of Farlo, *Romanism*, p. 57.

favour of the teaching of our Lord and His
Apostles.

The second article of the Creed is, if possible,
more effective still in closing the Bible to the
people.   In this the believer admits the Holy
Scriptures "in the same sense as the Church hath
held and doth hold them," and promises "not
to interpret them except according to the unanimous consent of the Fathers."   How can
people unacquainted with Hebrew, Greek, or Latin
know what is in the Scriptures unless trans-
lations into the common languages are made?
How can they learn "the sense in which the
Church has held them?"   And seeing that in
different ages, and in distant places, most contradictory interpretations have been given, how
can they interpret them according to the unanimous consent of the Fathers?   It is a life's work
to read what the Fathers have taught, and
absolutely impossible to harmonize their teaching.   If all the passages on which the Fathers
have expressed contradictory opinions were cut
out of the Bible there would be little left.   The
reading of the Scriptures, it is true, is not forbidden : but this article has made intelligent
reading of them impossible.   It is not surpris-

ing that most of the members of the Church of
Rome read other religious works in preference
to the book God has given.

In harmony with the spirit of this creed,
has been the practice of the Romish Church.
As far as possible, resistance has been offered to
the popular demand for the Bible in a known
language; and at first translators and printers
had to work in secret as they were in danger of
death. Where the powers to persecute has
been taken out of the hands of the Church,
and the Bible has been put into circulation,
the priests exert their great influence to dis-
courage the people from reading it. In Spain,
Italy, and other countries where the power of
the Pope is still great, the ignorance of the
teaching of God's word is profound and
universal. The efforts of the Bible Society and
similar institutions are openly anathematized,
and the books obtained through their agency
are demanded by the priests that they may be
destroyed. It seems as if there is a fear that if
the Bible were read, the people would learn that
the way to the Father is open to all, without the
intervention of the priest; and that it would be
difficult to harmonize much that is taught and

done with precepts of Jesus Christ and His Apostles.

As in India, suitably written books are given to those from whom the Vedas have been withheld, the Romish church has not been slack in providing books for those from whom the Bibie is withheld. What is their character? The teaching, for the most part, is such as to lead away the thoughts and devotion from a Father infinite in mercy, goodness, love ; from a Saviour whose compassion prompted Him to seek out the suffering and the sinful, that He might save and comfort, and lead the people to put their trust in, and centre their affections upon the Virgin Mary and a host of saints, in order to secure their intercession with God. It is in these books that the peculiar teaching of the Romish Church is given; that which finds its authority in the traditions rather than in the Bible. A study of these works will show clearly the expediency of discouraging the circulation and study of the word of God. Strange to say, the Fathers are practically unanimous on this point : that the Scriptures are the sole authority on questions of doctrine ; they fully admit that they themselves are fallible men.

If the Holy Scriptures are divinely inspired, is it not strange that they should be couched in terms that the pious, though ignorant, readers cannot understand them? Early in the 4th century, writing on this question Lactantius asks "Is not God the Creator of the mind, and voice and tongue able to speak clearly? Undoubtedly He is; and by His divine providence He wills that His divine truth should be devoid of all disguise, that all might understand what was spoken alike to all." History repeats itself. Our Saviour condemned the practice of those who in His day made the commandments of God of none effect by their traditions. It seems to be one of the greatest, perhaps the fundamental error of Rome to refuse the Scriptures to the people, or at any rate to put obstacles in the way of those who would study them.

Occasionally Popes have highly commended the study of the Scriptures. Thus Gregory XIII. writing soon after the Council of Trent—in a letter addressed to the King of France, which was prefixed to the royal edition of the French Bible, says, "every ground of our salvation and happiness is contained in it, nothing can be more excellent than the reading of these books nothing more fruitful, nothing better adapted to every race of mankind. In a similar sense Pius VI., in his letter to Archbishop Martini commending his well-known translation of the Vulgate into Italian, writes :—" The Scriptures are those abundant fountains which ought to be open for all, in order that they may drink in both holiness of life and doctrine," adding " and you have done opportunely in putting forth in our own tongue the divine letters, in order that they may be within reach of all." [1] And yet, strange to say, a lady in the diocese of Arezzo very soon after this letter was written, was threatened with excommunication by her priest for reading a portion of Scripture daily from this very translation ! The prohibition, rather than the politely written letter was more in harmony with the principles and practice of the Papacy when it is remembered that Clement XI., in 1713, solemnly condemned the following self evident propositions as they seem to us, which were propounded by Quesnel :—

"It is useful and necessary, at all times and in all places, and for all kinds of persons to

[1] *Romanism*, p. 80.

study the Scriptures, and to understand its spirit, its piety, and its mysteries.

"The holy obscurity of the Word of God is not a reason for any man to dispense with reading it.

"To take from the hands of Christians the Holy Bible, or to close it to them by taking away from them the means of its interpretation, is to shut up from them the very mouth of Christ.

"To prohibit the reading of the Scriptures, and particularly the Gospels, is to deny the use of light to the children of light, and to make them suffer a kind of excommunication."[1]

Erasmus has put the case perhaps as clearly and forcibly as anyone since his time. "Let us consider what kind of hearers Christ Himself had. Were they not a promiscuous multitude, among them the blind, the halt, beggars, publicans centurions, workmen, and even boys? If Christ did not exclude them from hearing His voice, neither will I exclude them from reading His books. I would that they were translated into every language. For Christ desired His holy

---

[1] *Romanism*, p. 80.

philosophy to be propagated as widely as possible. As He died for all, He wished to be known by all." [1]

The idea of " reserving " knowledge from the masses which may be given to a favoured few was doubtless suggested by what were termed "mysteries" in pagan worship. This hidden doctrine was carefully concealed until a process of initiation was effected ; and the initiated were prevented by the administration of a dreadful oath from divulging it to others. These mysteries were connected with several deities, and it was only after a somewhat lengthened waiting, that the coveted knowledge was imparted. In the early ages of the Church, as long as the departure from apostolic teaching was slight, the study of the Scriptures was not forbidden ; but when the deviation was pronounced, the light of revelation was inconvenient. The darkness was congenial when the Church's deeds became evil. From the day the Bible became dangerous, the declension of the Church became rapid. For by the very necessity of closing its sacred pages, confession was made

---

[1] *Romanism*, p. 85.

that human invention was trusted rather than the revelation of God. In forbidding the people to read it, the priests themselves closed their eyes to the truth and judicial blindness followed as a natural result.

CHAPTER III

SALVATION

IN the all-important matter of salvation, the departure of the Church of Rome from the simplicity of apostolic practice has been most marked. The gaoler at Philippi furnishes a typical illustration of what was common then. In his distress he cried, "What must I do to be saved?" The answer was given in a single sentence, "Believe in the Lord Jesus Christ." The same night he and his household received baptism, and was assured of his salvation, for "he rejoiced in God with all his house." There was the earnest question of an inquirer, the answer of an apostle, and the immediate enjoyment of the blessing sought. But now, alas, all this is changed. The obtaining of salvation, once so simple, is a most complicated business now. And when a man has followed the instructions of a priest, he cannot be certain that

he will enter heaven. The teaching of the
Council of Trent is clear on this:—"No man
can know with infallible assurance of faith, that
he has obtained the grace of God." Hence,
urged by fear of evil, those about to die have
given their goods, and after their death, their
surviving friends have impoverished themselves
in order to secure the help of priestly interces-
sions on their behalf.

India furnishes us with an illustration of the
way in which an interested priesthood has made
the way of salvation difficult, and the result
uncertain after all. Duties are multiplied,
each in turn declared to be necessary; and
though a life-time is spent in their discharge,
no assurance of salvation is given.

Every child is believed to be the direct gift
of a god: but this does not secure its well-
being. When only four days old another deity,
styled the Creator, must be approached with
gifts, in order that he may decree a life of
happiness, as its earthly career is then irrevoc-
ably fixed. At twelve years of age a guru or
confessor is appointed, who undertakes the
responsibility of the child's religious welfare,
and selects one of the many deities, as the

special object of its worship. Henceforth the
closest ties bind preceptor and pupil. It is
considered less dangerous to offend a god than
a guru, because this man is able to open or close
the gate of heaven for his disciples. When the
youth grows up to manhood, and is burdened
with a sense of sin, he is advised to bathe at
Saugor Island, where holy river and sea meet;
to visit Benares, the city specially sacred to the
great god ; to make a pilgrimage to Puri, the head
quarters of the worship of Jagannatha. Promises
are found in sacred books that those who perform these ceremonies will find salvation. But
though the condition is fulfilled, the blessing
is not found.

Even when a man has done all, there is no
peace. For it is taught that unless his descendants,
for generations, continue to authorize services on
his behalf, his spirit, even though in heaven, will
be in misery. If he be a special worshipper of
Siva, the great god, a sacred bull must be set
free to wander at will, damaging the growing
crops, or robbing shopkeepers of their grain.
At the funeral feasts, Brahmans and other castes
must be fed, that through their good offices, the
inhabitants of the spirit-world may welcome the

3

new arrival. At wedding and other important ceremonies, offerings must be made on their behalf. If these be neglected a man's own personal efforts will fail to ensure his salvation. And in all these rites the assistance of the priest is necessary.

This is paganism outside the Church; in principle the practice of the Roman Catholic Church does not greatly differ.

The first act necessary to salvation is Baptism. By a decree of the Council of Trent it is affirmed that "the Sacraments contain the grace which they signify, and confer that grace itself upon all who do not present a bar" or obstacle. According to this, the reception of the grace depends rather upon the priest conferring, than upon the people receiving. Under certain circumstances, the administration of Baptism is valid if performed by one not in priest's orders; provided that it was done with "the intention of doing what the Church does." But when a person from another communion joins that of Rome, although already baptized, the rite is again administered.

Next comes the Sacrament of Confirmation. By this the disciple is initiated into the mysteries of the Church, and comes under the influence of the Confessor. The chain is now forged which binds him to a fellow man, who professes to have the power to forgive, or to refuse the forgiveness of sin. In the confessional there is not a voluntary recital of offences, and the acceptance of what the priest considers an appropriate penance, or punishment; but a searching inquiry is made concerning the most sacred thoughts and desires. He who hears this confession speaks with divine authority; hence his immense influence over the penitents. Every means of bringing men into subjection to a priest seems to be in use. Salvation is so great a blessing; hell-fire so dreadful a doom, it is not surprising that people should live in dread of those in whose hand such momentous issues lie. The penance ordered, before absolution is granted, is said to be a compensation for the sin, as though the infinite mercy of God were insufficient. "We properly satisfy for our own sins, whilst Christ's satisfaction serves only to make it valid;"[1] a doctrine entirely opposed to the teaching of Jesus Christ Himself. He

---

[1] *Romanism*, p. 101,

taught that there was a full and free forgiveness for the penitent soul; His would-be exclusive teachers affirm that, in the true sense of the word, there is no pardon, seeing that every sinful act must bring upon the sinner its appropriate punishment. If penance is our equivalent for a sin, where is forgiveness?

The power of the priest to absolve has been carried to its logical conclusion. If the living can secure absolution, why not the dead? So when a man dies before the magical words "I absolve thee," are spoken in the sacrament of Extreme Unction, his friends can secure this boon for him. The priest asks the assembled friends if they wish the dead man to be absolved, and on their request, addressing the corpse, he says, "I absolve thee."[1] A case is cited of a baron who died excommunicated. After his death his case was reconsidered, as though he still lived, and absolution duly pronounced; and Pope Urban IV., ordered the absolution of the Emperor Henry to be declared after his death, or his body could not have been laid in consecrated ground.

Romanism, p. 100.

But the uncertainty of salvation, when it is made contingent upon the action of others, does not end here. In order to secure a happy entrance into heaven, the rite of Extreme Unction must be administered. When death seems near, this last solemn ceremony is considered necessary. The body is anointed with oil, professedly in accordance with the instruction in the Epistle of St. James, although the anointing there commended was to be employed as a means of securing the recovery of the sick; and the consecrated wafer is placed upon his tongue. Unless this is done, it is feared that the dying man's salvation is imperilled. Here again there is the necessity for the intervention of the priest; another obstacle is put in the way of the soul's direct communion with God. In principle this is exactly like the custom of the Hindus in removing their dying friends to the banks of a sacred stream, filling their lips with holy water, and placing a few grains of consecrated rice on their tongue.

And finally it is taught, that after death masses must be said for the repose of the soul, by which its sufferings in purgatory may be shortened and lessened. This doctrine is taught with the greatest earnestness, and in very similar terms to those employed by the pagans of India and China. At certain seasons of the year most impassioned addresses are delivered in the Churches, appealing to the love of the worshippers for friends departed. The pains of souls in the intermediate state are described in the strongest terms, as a means of inducing the living to arrange for masses on their behalf. Children are urged to save their parents from the pains of purgatory; and where no one specially dear may be in need, the general benevolence of the people is appealed to on behalf of those who may have no relatives sufficiently interested to perform this service on their behalf. It is distinctly taught that the living can secure their own salvation; but those who have passed away are entirely dependent on those still on earth. Did any one really believe that the saying of a mass would save a soul from the flames, what altar would be empty? The infallible Church has however limited the number to be offered by any priest to three a day.

From what has been said it will be seen how similar in principle is the paganism of the East and West. In place of the simple apostolic instruction "believe and be saved," an elaborate series of ceremonies is enjoined, for the right performance of which the repeated intervention of a priest is necessary. Whence came the additional services? Are they the natural development of the Master's and apostles' teaching? Or have we here the adoption of what was in vogue in the district where the recognised head of the Church held his courts and issued his commands?

The origin of the confessional is distinctly and undoubtedly pagan. The ceremony of initiation into the Church, with confession to a priest, was copied in almost every particular from the initiation into the "mysteries" of the gods of Greece and Rome. If further search be made it will be found that the original home of the practice was Babylon, where idolatry first arose. It was there that men turned aside from the worship of God, to adore the hosts of heaven, and afterwards the products of human imagination. And as at first this declension would have involved suffering at the hands of the faithful, the greatest secrecy was observed :—the doctrine and practice were only gradually taught to those who were considered suitable. By most stringent oaths, the new members were advanced from stage to stage. There were outward and public rites to which the general public were admitted, there were also secret and carefully concealed doctrine and practice with which the " initiated " only were made familiar. And along with the objects of worship, the peculiar ceremonies were carried from Babylon to Egypt, Greece, and Rome. So carefully kept were the secrets thus solemnly communicated that there is very little certainly known concerning them. For after a man forsook these societies, through respect to his oath or through fear of evil consequences from the gods, or those with whom he had been formerly associated, he would shrink from revealing what he had learned.

But enough is known to show that this was the model which was copied by the Christian leaders. The priest who initiated the members proposed certain questions to which answers were made in a set form. These questions were of a very personal character, not unlike those in use in the Roman Catholic confessional to-day. The main object of these searching examinations was to make the priest familiar with the secret life of the candidate, that he might render him obedient to his will. "Their silence, in regard to everything they were commanded to keep secret, was secured both by the fear of the penalties threatened to a perjured revelation, and by the general confession of the aspirant after initiation; a confession which caused them greater dread of the indiscretion of the priest, than gave him reason to dread their indiscretion."[1] Can there be any doubt as to the original of the confessional? In its present form it is in principle identical with the old pagan practice.

And with the confessional came the idea of priestly absolution. The one who examined the candidate and administered the oath, decided whether he was to be admitted or rejected; or whether his admission was to be deferred. As great benefit was hoped for by the initiated,—they expected to be admitted into a state of friendly relation with the god by this process,—it can easily be understood that there was a strong desire on the part of many to secure this privilege. The power to admit or reject gave the hierophant immense influence.

[1] Potter's *Greek Antiquities*, vol. 1, 356.

So is it with the priest of the Romish Church. He professes to have the power to bind or loose, to open or close the gate of heaven.

The awful usurpation of the divine prerogative was not effected by a single effort. For centuries the phraseology employed was in the form of a prayer that God would absolve the penitent. As late as the 13th century, William of Auxerre, Bishop of Paris, and Cardinal Hugo strongly denounced the new formula in which the priest said, "I absolve thee," and declared that even the apostles did not employ such language. They affirmed that the innovation was not more than twenty years old.[1]

In the case of Extreme Unction the origin is clearly traced. This important ceremony consists in the anointing of the body of the dying person with oil, and the placing of the consecrated host upon the tongue. The modern pagan counterpart to the latter is seen in the giving of Ganges water to dying Hindus; the river being regarded as a goddess, as the wafer is declared to be part of the body and blood of the Divine Saviour. When a person was about

[1] *Romanism*, p. 99.

to consult an oracle, *i.e.* to enter into the presence of a god, it was customary to anoint the body with oil. This custom arose from the fact that an olive branch was a recognised symbol of the Messiah or Mediator in the old Babylonian system, and was carried from there to Rome. By this anointing the intercession of the Mediator was sought. The reference to the Epistle of St. James was evidently an after thought. The question of Purgatory will be considered later on.

When considering the condition of those trusting in Jesus Christ, the language of the New Testament is clear and full: "There is therefore now no condemnation to those who are in Christ Jesus." Who can separate the believer from his Saviour? The cruelty of heathenism in the East, and of paganized heathenism in the West, is seen in the way it holds its adherent in perpetual doubt concerning the future, in order that they may have recourse to its nostrums, administered by its priests. Rome's "grand object has always been to keep the souls of its votaries away from direct and immediate intercourse with a loving and merciful Saviour, and to inspire a sense of the necessity

of human mediation. Considering the preten-
sions which it makes to absolute infalli-
bility, and the supernatural powers which it
attributes to its priests in regard to regeneration,
and the forgiveness of sin, it might have been
supposed, as a matter of course, that all its
adherents would have been encouraged to rejoice
in the assurance of their personal salvation.
But the very contrary is the fact. Perpetual
doubt to his life's end is inculcated as a duty."[1]

[1] *The Two Babylons*, p. 215

CHAPTER IV

GOOD WORKS AND INDULGENCES

As on the important subject of salvation there is a marked departure from the simplicity of Scripture, and the adoption of what was common in paganism, the same process is evident when we examine the answer given to the question, " How can man be just before God ? "

The infallible Church teaches that the grace received at Baptism imparts a special character to a man's conduct ; that what was inherently good becomes of still greater value through this grace. The Holy Spirit leads to a life of faith in and obedience to God, which in some cases is equal to God's requirements, in others it may be above or below that standard. When it is above what is necessary for the salvation of the individual, it is termed meritorious, and being added to the merit inhering in the Virgin Mary, and to the infinite merit of the Saviour's suffer-

ings, forms a fund which can be drawn upon
for those who need it. From this inexhaustible
treasury, indulgences are granted, by which
punishments are remitted in this life, and the
pains of Purgatory modified.

The accumulation of "merit" is the aim of
many Hindus. At their shrines are saints, who,
by the endurance of intense physical pain, are
endeavouring to acquire merit, which, they admit, is not necessary to salvation. This can be
used for themselves or for others. According
to their belief, conduct is divided into two classes,
necessary and meritorious. Amongst the necessary duties are the observance of the rules
relating to their own caste, and abstinence from
certain articles of food. To disregard these
duties, a man brings upon himself exclusion
from the society of his fellow castemen here, a
more or less lengthy residence in hell, and the
re-appearance on earth in a lower caste than
that of which he was a member in his present
life. In some of their religious books is a long
list of actions, with their appropriate penance
or punishment. And, on the other side, is a
list of "good works," which may be used in
liquidating the debts incurred according to the

list of offences.   Amongst these are pilgrimages
to shrines ; gifts to the gods without any expectation of special benefit in return ; acts of
worship without the desire for personal gifts ;
the erection of temples, presents to Brahmans
and other similar deeds.   By such works a man
may more than balance his sins, and the surplus
can be employed in lengthening his stay in
heaven, raising his position in his next earthly
life, and benefitting his ancestors and others
whose conduct fell short of what was necessary
to salvation.

In China a similar system is in vogue.   There
the list of virtues and vices is drawn up more
elaborately.   The virtue acquired in a given
year can be carried forward ; and the debt of
any year wiped out by extra deeds in the year
following.   The merit can be expended on
securing the welfare here and hereafter of him
who obtains it, or be applied to others.

The similarity between this and what is common in the Romish Church is very striking.   It
is in her teaching on the question of justification
that the whole structure is built.   This we shall
now consider.

At the Council of Trent (1545-1563) this

doctrine was settled. The view which was accepted had been held for some time previously by many, though by no means all those present. Cardinal Seripandi opened the discussion, but unfortunately his views were repudiated. "The state of the question is this :— Whether we who are justified before the Divine tribunal, are to be judged only by the righteousness of our own works, proceeding out of the charity (grace) which is in us, or by a two-fold righteousness, our own, and the righteousness of Christ supplying our imperfections. They say we ought to reply to these questions not speculatively but practically. Let the sinner be arraigned before the tribunal of God, and asked ' whether he will be judged only by his own righteousness, and rely upon that, or will supply his imperfections by the righteousness of Christ.' [1] It is certain that when a test of this practical character is applied, few would be bold enough to trust in their own works alone, but would fall back on the merits of the Saviour. Hence others arguing on the same side said, " No man, when he is dying, takes refuge in his own

[1] *Romanism*, p. 111.

inherent righteousness, nor in the righteousness
of his past life, nor in his good works, but in
the passion of Christ and His mercy.   Therefore
our own inherent righteousness is insufficient to
constitute us righteous before the tribunal of
Christ."[1]   Another great dignity of the Church,
Cardinal Contarini, who died before the Council
had completed its labours, writes, "We see by
experience that holy men, the more they ad-
vance in holiness, so much the less are pleased
with themselves, and therefore so much the
more discover their need of Christ.   Hence
they forsake themselves, and rely on Him alone."
And in another place he declares, "this is the
received doctrine in the Christian Church; this
it is to be truly a Christian—to know well our
own weakness and to flee by faith to Christ;
to put all our hope in Him, distrusting our own
weakness.   Of this doctrine the Epistles of
Paul, of this the Gospels themselves, of this all
the Scriptures are full."   And again, "As we
have all sinned in Adam, and all deserve death
in him, so all our obedience is in Christ, and all
our deserts in Him."[2]

[1] *Romanism* p. 113.   [2] Ibid, p. 114.

4

Although such opinions were held and fear-lessly expressed by many, unfortunately they did not prevail. The leaven of heathenism had done its work, and the majority accepted "human inventions" in place of the precepts of Holy Scripture. " The Catholic position is this—that there is one single righteousness which is inherent to us, or rather which forms us whether it be grace or charity, by which everyone who is righteous is righteous, as St. Augustine testifies; through which one righteousness, our sins, are wiped away, and we are adopted among the children of God."[1] In its 32nd Article the Council of Trent anathematizes those who say that " the good works of a justified man are so far the gifts of God, that they are not also the good merits of the justified man himself, and that the justified person by the good works which he has done through the grace of God, and by the merits of Christ, does not truly merit increase of grace, and eternal life." Dr. Di Bruno teaches that " regeneration, and therefore justification and pardon of sin given for the first time, are clearly attached by

[1] *Romanism*, p. 115.

our Lord to the Sacrament of Baptism, and has plainly and peremptorily attached the pardoning of sin, at other times to the sacramental absolution of the priest, and not to mere trusting; though hope and trust in God is in itself one of the necessary dispositions never to be omitted on coming to the Sacrament of penance as the Catholic Church teaches."[1]   The Council of Trent distinctly teaches that " Men are not justified by the imputation of Christ's righteousness alone."

A sentence or two from more recent writers will give the present form of this great doctrine in the Church of Rome.   " We do as truly and properly merit rewards when we do well, as we do merit punishment when we do ill.   Our good works do merit eternal life *condignly*, not only by reason of God's covenant and acceptation, but also by reason of the work itself.[2]   Such are the words of Cardinal Bellarmine.   Vasquez goes a step farther.   " Seeing the works of good men do merit eternal life, there is no need that any condign merit, such as that of Christ, should

---

[1] *Primer of Roman Catholicism*, p. 115.

[2] *Romanism*, p. 116.

interpose, to the end that eternal life might be rendered to them." Strange to say although in life Bellarmine had expressed his views as above, when he came to die he expresses his faith in quite another fashion. In his will he writes, " I pray that God may admit me among the number of His saints and elect, not weighing my merits, but pardoning my offences.' The practical testing of opinion by death showing, in his case as in others, that it is God's infinite mercy rather than their own meritorious deeds that affords a truer defence, a safer shelter.

From what has been said, it will be seen the Church of Rome teaches that the justification of the soul is secured by the use of two means ; the merits of Jesus Christ obtained by the exercise of faith ; and the righteousness which, inheres in human souls, or which is produced by, or flows from some special grace. But this second ground of salvation, is of very variable quality and amount. In some it more nearly approaches perfection than others. Some therefore may have a surplus of merit, others be more or less deficient. Can the good works, which are over and above what is necessary in the superlatively good, be utilized for the benefit of those who fall short? This transfer of merit is openly advocated.

Good actions are divided into two classes, those necessary to salvation, and those above what is necessary. To these latter the term "works of supererogation" is given. Some actions are commanded, and are therefore necessary to salvation, others are counselled, and are desirable only. The authority for this distinction is based on the conversation of our Lord with the rich young ruler who asked, "What good thing shall I do, that I may have eternal life?" Jesus enumerated the chief commandments, and when the inquirer replied, "All these things have I kept from my youth up, what lack I yet?" Jesus answered, "if thou wilt be perfect, go and sell all that thou hast and give to the poor, and thou shalt have treasure in heaven." It is affirmed that our Lord made a distinction between what was necessary to salvation, and what would give something more than mere salvation, treasure in heaven, which could be utilized for the good of others, as his earthly treasures might benefit the poor. These works are not said to be inherently better than those regarded as necessary, nor that they are performed independently of God-given grace; but they being beyond what will secure the personal salvation of him who performs them, can be made use of for those whose attainments may be a little below the necessary. It is as though a thousand marks are declared to be necessary for candidates to pass an examination. One man obtains fifteen hundred; the five hundred are then available for those who have failed to secure a thousand.

When it was accepted that it was possible for some to secure a greater merit than was actually required for themselves, the question arose as to what use could be made of this spiritual wealth. He who earned it did not need it; and it was far too valuable to be lost. Then came in the doctrine of indulgences, for the purchase of which this merit of the Saints, added to that of the Virgin and her Divine Son, was available. The purchase, however, was not made from those whose piety had secured it but from the Church represented by Pope and Priests to whose credit it was placed in heaven's treasury. In the present age an indulgence is said to be a remission of the temporal punishment which a sin merits, after the sinner has obtained divine forgiveness; and the punishment, from which it secures deliverance, though generally granted to the living, may be, and frequently is, extended to those who are passing through the cleansing fires of purgatory.

The origin of this monstrous system was very simple and almost innocent. In the early Church, the greatest effort was made to secure the purity of the members. They separated themselves from a corrupt society; it was therefore a matter of supreme importance that their life should show the beneficial influence of the gospel. When therefore any member fell into open sin, he was cut off for a longer or shorter period from the Services or Sacraments of the Church. This deprivation of a privilege was regarded as an expiation; a punishment inflicted by the visible Church after the offender had obtained divine forgiveness. Sin was regarded as an offence against God whose pardon had to be sought, and as a crime against His visible Kingdom, which had to be expiated by punishment. It was a common practice for these penalties pronounced by the Church, to be lightened or shortened in response to a request from the Confessors and Martyrs, whose fidelity to the faith, and suffering for conscience sake had raised them to a higher level than those who had not thus endured. Their super-excellence was available to make up for the lack of excellence of those who had fallen. Of course this freedom from merited punishment was bestowed only on those whose penitence was manifest; and in many cases penitence had to be accompanied by good deeds. The next step was a disastrous one, and some time elapsed before it was generally accepted. The "good works" prescribed as the necessary accompaniment of penitence, could be commuted by a money-payment for a specified object; and then, later still, by the payment of money to the Church, without its being ear-marked, and might be spent in any way the priests might wish. This opened a broad way for corruption. Though the thing signified was in practice long before, it was not until the 11th century that the term Indulgence was in common use. In the time of the Crusades, service in these holy wars, or assisting them by gifts of money, purchased a full indulgence from all kinds of penance. And, by this means, many a sinner secured salvation from the penalties of sin they might afterwards commit as of sins of which they were already guilty. At first local Bishops had the power to grant partial, and even plenary or full indulgences to those within their own diocese; but Innocent III. reserved for the Popes the power to grant the fuller forgiveness. Gradually the misuse of their power increased, until it had assumed such vast dimensions as to scandalise the more thoughtful and earnest of the flock, and was the occasion of the rise of the Reformation in Europe. It was one of many evils, perhaps the most glaring, which set afire the combustible materials accumulating for centuries.

The creed of Pope Pius IV. expressly declares that "the power of indulgences has been left in the Church by Christ, and their use by Christian people is of a most saving character." Though this was the authoritative statement of the Church, at the time of the Reformation most opposite views were held. In fact, in the Council where the question was discussed, some were almost as outspoken as Luther himself in their opposition to this dreadful doctrine. Nevertheless the majority silenced those who objected, and belief in the efficacy of indulgences was authoritatively affirmed. When the consideration of this question came on, Cardinal Cajetan, who held the brief in their favour, boldly marshalls the objections that could be raised against them. He represents an opponent declaring, that as no one had ever performed more good works than were due to God, there was consequently no surplus available for others ; that even martyrs for the truth, who were commonly believed to be the richest in this wonder-working merit, simply did their duty by remaining faithful unto death ; and that as St. Augustine taught, it was the duty of all saints to pray " Forgive us our sins," thus expressing, that they as well as others were in need of pardon. And that supposing a saint could perform good works above, what was necessary for himself, they could not avail for others defects. Having thus voiced the objections of his opponents, when we should have expected him to admit their force and validity, he falls back on the unlimited power of the Pope to proclaim their efficacy as a sufficient answer. And further, after rehearsing the objection that the Saviour committed to the Pope power to forgive the sins of the living only, the Cardinal's answer was, that the Pope's declaration in his letter of indulgence proved that he could open

the Kingdom of heaven through the merits of
Christ and the Saints, to the souls in Purgatory,
taking them out of the pains which hindered
them from entering the kingdom of heaven.
This same Cardinal in the last work he wrote,
commenting on 2 Peter ii. 3, "and through
covetousness shall they with feigned words make
merchandise of you," says "not far from such as
these are those preachers who abuse the devotion
of Christian people for gain ; who ignorantly or
rashly dare to preach that those who pay a
carline, or a ducat, for what is called plenary
absolution are in the same state as if they were
newly baptized, and in the same manner that
they can free a soul from Purgatory ; for these
are monstrous things and traffickings with
Christian people.   The Christian religion knows
no such figments ; they are inventions of those
who through covetousness with feigned words
make merchandise of Christians, abusing them
for gain."[1]   Strange language from one who
had argued in favour of the use of indulgences,
and was well aware to what extent the Pope
had profited by their sale!

[1] *Romanism*, p. 235, 6.

In 1350, this theory was formulated, and issued with the authority of Pope Clement VI· After referring to the death of Christ for the salvation of the world he says, " Wherefore from hence, in order that the mercy of so great an effusion of blood should not be void or superfluous, He acquired a treasure for the Church militant, working as a pious father, to lay up a store for his sons. Which treasure He did not hide in a napkin, or bury in a field, but committed to be dispensed through St. Peter, the key-bearer of heaven, and his successors, his vicars upon earth. To add to which heap of treasure, the merits of the Blessed Virgin, and of all the elect from the first to the last are known to give their assistance, so that none need fear its consumption or diminution."[1]

The indulgences granted in consideration of this treasury of merit, are either partial or plenary. The lessser gift is when a part only of the penalty is remitted, the plenary when there is a full and complete deliverance. It was in the year 1095 that the larger gift came into use. The object of this great offer was

[1] *Romanism*, p. 239.

an inducement to nobles and their retainers to volunteer for the Crusades. This was an agreeable method, for professional soldiers, of obtaining a discharge of their obligations to God and the Church. As the indulgence had retrospective and prospective effect ; as it was declared to be efficacious in saving a soul from the pains of Purgatory, as well as from ecclesiastically imposed penance, it is not surprising that it was effectual in leading some of the worst men to volunteer for the wars against the Moors.

There is another form in which this treasure of merit can be drawn upon, *viz.* by securing immunity from punishment by the purchase of what is called a dispensation. Under Papal authority, a catalogue of crimes is published, in which the money price is quoted for payment of which an absolution, or license can be obtained. Almost every sin that can be named has its price. By this means a court is provided in which the rich can purchase freedom to gratify the desires of an evil heart. When it is remembered that these indulgences and dispensations, are said to avail not only before the bar of the Church, but at the judgment seat of the All-righteous God ; that by the authority of the

Vicar of Christ a man can be delivered from the just judgment of the Almighty, there seems to be no greater departure from the truth imaginable. To exaggerate the evil of this teaching is impossible.

In 1552, the Roman Catholic Princes of Germany drew up a memorial of grievances in which they complain not only of the heavy drain on their purses which the purchase of indulgences makes, but of the lack of piety induced by their frequent sale. They speak of the people, by their means, being encouraged to commit all kinds of sins, when they know they can purchase immunity from punishment in this life and the next.

A strong indictment against the multiplication of these deliverances from the due punishment of sin is made by Dean Alford in his *Letters form Abroad.* " By visiting the Church of Santa Croce in Gerusalemme on the second Sunday in Advent, may be gained 11,000 years of indulgence and remission of all ones sins. By visiting that of SS. Cosmas and Damian in the Forum any day a 1,000 years, and on the day of the Stations, 10,000 years. By kissing the foot of the idol in St. Agostino once every day, 100 years of indulgence may be gained : so that if a devout Roman Catholic choose to pass in his walk every day for a year these two last Churches he might gain at St. Agostino 36,500, and at SS. Cosmas and Damian 365,000 years remission from Purgatory—in all 401,500 years for every day of his life from these two Churches only. It is no exaggeration to say that this number might easily be multiplied ten-fold without entailing any onerous duty. Percy gives an authorised measure of the Virgin's foot from her real shoe, on which is inscribed that Pope John XXII. conceded 300 years (in the German authorised edition of the same it is 700) of indulgence to whosoever should kiss the measure and recite three Ave Marias. This was confirmed by Pope Clement VIII. in 1603, and was extended to any similar measures taken from the original one ; adding that it is applicable to souls in Purgatory. So that any devout German, without stirring from his chair, might, supposing three Ave Marias to occupy five minutes, gain in one hour of each day of his life, 8,400 years of indulgence, or by this means alone each year upwards of 3,000.000." [1]

_____

[1] *Manual of Roman Catholicism*, p. 103.

Where are we to look for the origin of this
dreadful doctrine, with its wonderful development?   Not to the New Testament certainly,
In the teaching of our Lord, as in that of His
Apostles, we shall look in vain for any counten-
ance to the idea that a man may acquire merit
which can be made available for the short-
comings of others.   The opposite of this is
clearly taught by them.   When a man has done
his best he is but an unprofitable servant, he has
done no more than his duty.   And in the
parable of the Virgins the wise who had oil for
their lamps, are represented as having none over
to supply the needs of others.   The Apostles
made no claim to possess the power of setting
men free from merited punishment who had
paid them for this service.   Without doubt we
have here a relic or a revival of Paganism of a
very pronounced type, which was once common
in the city and country where this abomination
had its rise, and which has profited so largely
by it.

The proof of this statement is most convincing.
In the *Eleusinian Mysteries*, the model of
most others, " one of the great objects was the
presenting to fallen man the means of his return

to God.   These means were the cathartic or
purifying virtues, by the exercise of which a
corporeal life was to be vanquished.   Accordingly the mysteries were termed 'perfections,'
because they were supposed to induce to
perfectness of life.   Those who were purified by
them were said to be brought to perfection."—
In the *Metamorphoses of Apuleius*, who was
himself initiated in the mysteries of Isis, we find
this goddess represented as saying to the hero,
" If you shall be found to deserve the protection
of my divinity by sedulous obedience, religious
devotion, and inviolable chastity, you shall be
sensible that it is possible for me, and me alone,
to extend your life beyond the limits that have
been appointed to it by your destiny,"[1]   And
when the same individual has received proof of
the favour of the deity, the onlookers express
their congratulations in these terms :—" Happy
by Hercules! and thrice blessed he to have
merited, by the innocence and probity of his
past life, such special patronage of heaven."   In
Egypt the formulæ of the funeral ceremonies
were similar to those in the Romish Church.

[1] Hyslop's *Two Babylons*, p. 209.

5

The deceased is represented as asking for admission into the company of the Gods on the ground that he has merited this favour by his obedience and service. There Anubis was said to weigh the action of men and so decide their fate ; in Rome the Archangel Michael discharges this duty.

Naturally men feared to die when uncertain as to the result of their life assize. This caused them to avail themselves of the help of the priest in death, and to arrange for his further help after they had passed away. It is this which give Rome's priests such awful power over her people. " In a famous letter of Pere le Chaise, confessor of Louis XIV. of France, giving an account of the method he employed to gain his consent to the revocation of the Edict of Nantes, we see how the fear of the scales of St. Michael operated in bringing about the desired result. " Many a time since," says the accomplished Jesuit, referring to an atrocious sin of which the king had been guilty, " many a time since when I have been at confession, I have shook hell about his ears, and made him sigh, fear, and tremble, before I would give him absolution. By this I saw he had still an inclination to me and was ere long to be under my government. So I set the baseness of the action before him by telling the whole story, and how wicked it was, and that it could not be forgiven till he had done some good action to balance that and expiate the crime. Where-upon he at last asked me what he must do? I told him that he must root out all the heretics from his kingdom." Thus, as a work of merit to outweigh a grave crime, the weak king in the hand of a cunning confessor was induced to authorize the massacre of the Huguenots.

CHAPTER V

PURGATORY

THE term Purgatory signifies a state or place of cleansing. According to Roman Catholic teaching, those who enter it, though saved from the eternal punishment of hell, are not sufficiently pure to enter into the presence of God. Their mortal sin is forgiven, but their so-called venial sin remains, and must be got rid of by the fires of Purgatory. This painful experience can be modified in fierceness and duration by the prayers and gifts of the living rather than by the sufferers themselves.

The present day belief is thus expressed in the Creed of Pope Pius IV. " I constantly hold that there is a Purgatory, that the souls therein detained are assisted by the suffrages of the faithful." In greater fulness the doctrine is stated by one of Rome's learned teachers :—" There is a Purgatory, that is to say, a place or state, where souls departing this life, with the remission of sin, as to the guilt, or eternal pain, but yet liable to some temporal punishment, still remaining due ; or not perfectly freed from the blemish of some defects, which we call venial sin, are purged before their admittance into heaven, where nothing that defileth can enter. Such souls so detained in Purgatory, being the living members of Christ Jesus, are relieved by the prayers and suffrages of their fellow members here on earth."

It will be noticed that sin is separated into two classes, mortal and venial. Whilst mortal sin consigns the sinner to eternal damnation, venial sin can be acted upon by the fires of Purgatory. There has been great diversity of opinion as to what sin is mortal, what venial. The common belief is that any sin is venial when it is seen to be sin, and there is penitence of heart concerning it ; whilst persistence in evil is mortal and unpardonable. Some affirm that mortal sin deprives the guilty of sanctifying grace, whilst venial sin only weakens it. This is another way of saying that persistency in evil renders salvation impossible, because there is no desire for this great blessing, nor any effort to secure it; whilst a temporary fall may coincide with what is, on the whole, a life of faith and obedience. It is for such people that a place of purging is considered necessary before they "are meet for the inheritance of the Saints in light."

The great evil connected with this subject is not so much the belief that an intermediate state is necessary, as that the purifying process is said to be largely affected by the gifts and prayers of others, rather than by those who are undergoing it. The rich can secure the saying of numbers of masses on their behalf; the poor have no such remedy. It is true the charitably disposed are earnestly entreated to pay for masses to help the poor, as in Protestant Churches they are asked to support missions amongst the heathen.

The saying of masses is the means by which the pains of Purgatory can be modified. It is as though God were a hard creditor, who, whilst forgiving the greater part of a debt demands an equivalent for the rest. The sacrifice represented by the payment of money is the asset available for the balance, and can be paid before a man's death, or by his surviving friends. Strange to say the Canon of the Mass used for the dead excludes the idea of Purgatory, and speaks of those on whose behalf it is offered as " sleeping the sleep of peace." " Remember also, Lord, Thy servants and hand-maids who have gone before us with the sign of faith, and sleep in peace. To them, Lord, and to all who rest in Christ, grant, we beseech Thee, a place of refreshment, of light, and peace,"[1] In a tract printed in 1497 on " The value of Masses," the writer clearly points out the uselessness of those that are offered by the living for the dead, although he was a priest of the Church. " One mass celebrated for you whilst living will profit you more than a hundred after your death ; one little prayer you now offer will be more useful to you than all the psalm singing of the monks will then be ; one sigh or tear you pour forth for your sins now, profits you more than all the groanings and sobs of monks and mourners." Alas ! this was the voice of one drowned by the shouts of a multitude. The profits arising from the appeals to the fears and affections of the faithful were too remunerative for a general reform to be effected.

[1] *Romanism*, 179.

The celebration of a mass is, professedly, the offering of the body and blood of our Lord to save a sinner from merited punishment. And yet one such sacrifice is not deemed sufficient. They are multiplied indefinitely, and continued for many years. Surely if the one offering of Jesus Christ was enough to save a world from the greater condemnation of hell, one mass ought to suffice to save a soul from the penalty imposed by the Church. In some Churches, the special masses which have been paid for are so numerous that it is impossible for them to be celebrated; hence the ordinary celebrations have to do double duty for the living and for the souls in Purgatory. In the Archdiocese of Vienna in 1787, the numbers of masses for the dead was 97,000, requiring more than three hundred priests daily to perform them. In one Church—St. John and St. Paul in Venice, the unperformed masses due at that time amounted to 16,400.[1] These had all been paid for, as a means of lessening the sufferings of those who had been saved by Jesus Christ, but who, at the hour of death, were not ready to enter His presence.

[1] *Romanism* p. 184.

What a slur this practice casts upon the justice
and mercy of God, and upon the saving work of
His dear Son, which has to be supplemented
by the sufferings of those who died trusting in
Him, and by the prayers and gifts of their surviving friends. Uncertain as to their parents fate,
affectionate children have impoverished themselves to assist them in their hour of suffering.
And it is supposed that this help will be needed
year after year. " The doctrine and invention
of Purgatory became a most forcible engine to
draw the people's money. For when men were
made to believe, that, after death, their souls
would enter into a region of fire, to suffer long
and bitter torment, to be purged and fitted for
the region of bliss ; but to be eased there, and
the sooner released, according to the number
of masses and prayers made on their behalf here,
people were put upon it to make the best pro-
vision they could in their lifetime, or, at least
at death, that such helps and means should be
used on their behalf, as they might reasonably
reckon upon a short and tolerable continuance
there."[1] It is with Romanism, as with heathen

[1] " On the intolerable charge of Popery to this Nation,"
Stavely quoted in *Romanism*, p. 184.

systems where similar faiths are held, the profit made by the priest casts suspicion upon it. The enormous amount of money received from the bequests of the dead and the gifts of the living on their behalf, impells the belief that it is a human invention; but when it is looked at in the light of our Lord's teaching, it is so opposed to the spirit of His gospel, that it is wonderful His professed disciples could accept the doctrine.

The contradictory teaching of authorities in Church doctrine on this important question is well worthy of notice. " I have sometimes endeavoured to understand the nature and import of this popish Purgatory, but could never yet meet with any satisfaction therein and to say the truth, the difference amongst the Papists are so many and irreconcileable, that they serve sufficiently, instead of all other reasons and arguments to confute it. First the place. Eckius will have it to be at the bottom of the sea, some will have it in Mt. Etna, and Bernardus de Bustis in a hill in Ireland. Next for the torments. Sir Thomas More will have them to be only by fire; but Fisher, his fellow sufferer, by fire and by water. Then for the executioners:—these differ no less again; for Bishop Fisher will have them to be holy angels, but Sir Thomas More to be the very devils. Then for the sins to be expiated ; some will have them to be venial only, and others say mortal too. And for the time for their continuance in that state, Dionysius the Carthusian extends it to the end of the world, whilst Dominicus a Soto limits it to ten years ; and others make it depend on the number of masses and offices that shall be done on their behalf, or if the Pope do but speak the word. Lastly for the extremity of their pains, Aquinas makes them as violent as those of hell ; but the Rhemists say that the souls there are in a very fine condition. But by all this uncertainty, and contrariety rather, of opinion, it may clearly be seen upon what weak foundation they have raised this building, which certainly would have fallen to the ground long ago, if it had not been for the profit which the popes, priests, and friars have raised by the fiction."[1]

The following may be taken as a specimen of the more popular style of teaching given by the priests of the Romish Church on this question.

[1] Stavely quoted in *Romanism*, p. 186.

It is taken from O'Sullivan's *Catholic History of Ireland* as a description of the Purgatory of St. Patrick. " There are numbers of men, whom no arithmetic can reckon up, all lying on the ground pierced through the body. They uttered hoarse cries of agony, their tongues cleaving to their jaws. They were buffeted by violent tempests, and shattered by repeated blows of devils. The devils drove them into another plain, horrible with exquisite tortures. Some, with iron chains about their necks and limbs, were suspended over fires, others were burned with red-hot cinders. Not a few were transfixed on the spits, and roasted, melted lead being poured into them. Alas for those who do not penance in this world." It will be remembered that this is not supposed to be a description of hell, but of that place to which souls saved from hell's torments are sent to get rid of the remains of sin which render them at present unfit to enter upon the bliss of heaven. Contrast this teaching with the word of Jesus to the thief upon the cross, " This day thou shalt be with me in Paradise," and with that of St. Paul where he declares that to be " absent from the body " is to be " present with the Lord." Does it not make God appear as a

relentless tyrant to inflict suffering such as this
upon those who have trusted in the Saviour?
It is a strange salvation if those, who accept it,
have to endure such pains before it can be
enjoyed.

In the teaching of Buddhism, on this question,
there is great similarity. At the entrance to the
temples are pictures, or life-size models representing men and women enduring the tortures of hell.
To this place all must go for a time, unless their
" merit " is greater than their sin. If a man during
his life, or, immediately on his death, his relatives
pay the price, the priests profess to secure a rapid
passage from hell to heaven, or, even to arrange for
him to go there direct. There are two powerful
motives impelling the survivors to hasten the
entrance into heaven of a deceased relative.
Love leads them to lighten the pain of one who
was dear, and fear drives them to do the same,
lest the unhappy spirit should bring evil upon
them.

But many have not the means or inclination
to incur the expense of these soul-saving ceremonies ; and their relatives are also lacking the
means of paying for them. These spirits may
be productive of evil to the community. To

prevent this, some who have no near relatives dependent on them, or may have more money than is required for them, will arrange for services on behalf of these friendless people.

In the Purgatory of the Papal Church, fire, literal fire is regarded as the chief means of purifying the soul; in the Buddhist hell, it is only one of many. The ingenuity of evil-minded priests has been employed in inventing forms of torture which are realistically represented in the temples. The main purpose of all this is, evidently, not to lead those who see them to live a good life, for by the performance of appropriate ceremonies they can obtain deliverance from sin's penalties; but to lead them to secure the assistance of the priests for their own benefit and for the benefit of others who have died.

Where did the Romish Church obtain the idea of Purgatory? It was a common idea among the heathen who crowded into the Church. Seeing the influence its acceptance gave to the priests of the pagan deities, the leaders of the Church deemed it politic to allow it to remain. In most ancient forms of religion there were similar beliefs and ceremonies. It was felt that in many cases men were not alto-

gether evil so as to deserve hell, nor sufficiently
pure to be admitted immediately into the abodes
of the gods. An intermediate state was therefore devised in which their salvation could be
completed, either by their own sufferings, or by
the efforts of their living friends, or by a combina-
tion of the two. Where men have been ignorant
of the infinite love of God in freely forgiving
the sinner, or where by the force of old religious
notions this truth has been obscured, they have
recource to this supplementary method of salvation. Thus Plato, speaking of the future judgment of the dead, holds out the hope of the final
deliverance of all, but maintains that, of those
who are judged, some must first " proceed to a
subterranean place where they shall sustain the
punishment they have deserved," others, in consequence of a favourable judgment, being elevated
at once to a celestial place, " shall pass their
time in a manner becoming the life they have
lived in a human shape." In pagan Rome it
was a common article of their religious belief
that it was only through a purgatory that they
could reach the heavenly fields. As a matter of
fact, Virgil is really the authority for much that
has come to be regarded as Christian truth.

Compare the following lines with what is written in acknowledged orthodox works of Roman Catholic doctors, and there can be little doubt on this question. Anchises is explaining to his son, Æneus, the process by which souls as they pass away from the world are freed from their impurities.

" Nor can the grovelling mind,
In the dark dungeons of the limbs confined,
Assert the native skies, or own its heavenly kind ;
Nor death itself can wholly wash their stains :
But long-contracted filth e'en in the soul remains.
The relics of inveterate vice they wear ;
And spots of sin obcene in every face appear.
For this are various penances enjoined ;
And some are hung to bleach upon the wind ;
Some plunged in waters, others purged in fires,
Till all the dregs are drained, and all the rust expires.
All have their manes, and these manes bear ;
The few so cleansed to these abodes repair,
And breathe in ample fields the soft Eliysian air.
Then are they happy, when by length of time
The scurf is worn away of each committed crime ;
No speck is left of their habitual stains,
But the pure ether of the soul remains." [1]

In Virgil other processes of cleaning are mentioned. In the teaching of the Romish Church fire is regarded as more common and more

[1] Dryden's *Æneid*, vi. 995.

powerful. Probably this arose from the Persian doctrine of the existence of a cleansing fire which was in the long run to burn up all evil. From thence the idea was carried to the West. In India Agni, the god of Fire, is said to be the Purifier, and the bodies of the Hindus are burned to ashes that by this process they may be freed from all impurity. In a hymn from one of the oldest sacred books addressed to him we have the following lines :—

" Preserve us Lord, thy faithful servants save
From all the ills by which our bliss is marred ;
Tower like an iron wall our homes to guard,
And all the boons bestow our hearts can crave,
And when away our brief existence wanes,
When we at length our earthly homes must quit,
And our freed souls to worlds unknown must flit,
Do thou deal gently with our cold remains,
And then, thy gracious form assuming, guide
Our unborn part across the dark abyss
Aloft to realms serene of light and bliss,
Where righteous men among the gods abide."

Such was the faith of a sister nation to Rome soon after she settled on the plains of India. Probably the idea was common to the people from whom the various branches of the Aryan family sprang. When the Western people came into the Christian Church, and became acquainted

6

with the Scriptural teaching concerning the awful purity of God, it is not difficult to understand how it came to be taught, that though faith in the Saviour had secured salvation from the eternal pains of hell, the sanctification of most being incomplete at death, must be somewhere perfected. Then came in the practice of "Extreme Unction," by which some of the evil of the soul could be removed, and the belief in an intermediate state where the good work could be completed. At first the teaching was comparatively harmless. No effort was made to extort money as a means of securing the happiness of the departed. A pious wish for the welfare of the dead gradually grew into formal prayers, and these developed into elaborate ceremonies which require the aid of a Priest.

Old stories connected with Hades of the pagan faith have been copied into Church teaching. In classic literature we read of men being carried into the Spirit world in seasons of madness or trance, and then allowed to return to relate their experience to the living. These stories reappear in later times, the actors having Christian names. Gregory the Great declared that a nobleman, named Stephen, died, and in Hades saw that many things which he had been taught were true, though he had not believed them. It was discovered that this Stephen was not the man summoned, but a smith bearing the same name. The smith died, the nobleman was permitted to return to the world. Of course his faith was confirmed by what he had seen and heard in Hades. By stories such as these the doubters were led to believe, and the stingy to become liberal.

CHAPTER VI

HOLY WATER

FROM the use of water in cleansing the body, it seems natural to adopt it as a symbol to signify the purifying of the soul from sin. In most religions it has been employed for that purpose. In or near the entrance of the temple, the laver of water was conspicuous. Here the travel stained worshipper could wash his feet before he crossed the threshold of the sacred building ; and as many came bare-footed, or wearing light sandals, it was a comforting, as well as cleansing act. The same was done on entering a house, and, in eastern lands, is practically the equivalent to the removal of the hat in the west.

The next step in the use of water as a religious rite, was to subject it to special treatment by which its purifying power was supposed to be increased. Then it was employed, not for the washing of the body, but to exert a miraculous cleansing of the moral nature. When the old temples were transformed into churches, the lavers remained in their place; when new ones were erected the vessel of holy water was not forgotten. The water was specially consecrated; and instead of the feet, hands, face being washed with it, a few drops were sprinkled on the worshippers. This wonder-working water was used in the Baptismal Font, at the consecration of buildings, and for purifying the congregation at certain holy seasons. The ceremony of charging the water with its special power, in the Romish Church takes place on the day after Good Friday, and is instructive. The following account is from " Foyes' Romish Rites."

There are three kinds of Holy Water. In the first, a little salt only is added, and is used in the consecration of buildings. In the second, salt, ashes, and wine are added, and is used at the consecration of altars. It is the third kind that with great solemnity is prepared on Holy Saturday, and is used for Baptism, and for sprinkling over the congregation. The ceremonies performed on this occasion are significant. The priest first divides the water in the font with his hand in the form of a cross. Then, touching it again with his hand, he expels demons and evil spirits. He breathes into it three times, and letting down the great Paschal candle into it, says " The might of the Holy Ghost descend into this fountain plenitude. This is repeated a second and a third time. Breathing into the water three times he says "Impregnate with regenerating efficacy the whole substance of this water," and removes the candle. A little oil, and stranger still, a little saliva is also mixed with it.

The water is now charged with the power to cleanse the soul from sin. What is the meaning of this consecration? It is said that when Linacre, a bigoted Romanist in the reign of Henry VIII., fell in with a copy of the New Testament, he said with an oath "either this Book is not true, or we are not Christians." The account of the various baptisms in the Scriptures does not lend much authority to ceremonies such as these. When St. John baptised the Saviour in the Jordan, there was no consecrated water available; and when St. Philip baptised the eunoch, and St. Paul baptised the gaoler at Philippi, it was ordinary, not holy water that was used. The use of holy water as a means of purifying the soul is essentially pagan.

Heathen poets had taught that infants uniniti-
ated into the mysteries of religion were classed
with suicides and consigned to hell. To save
them from this painful position, the merciful
spirit of Christianity led to the formation of the
doctrine of Baptismal Regeneration. The simple
initiatory right as instituted by the Saviour,
was charged with miraculous powers, and was
said to make those children of God, who,
naturally were children of the devil, whose
proper portion was the torment of hell. By the
act of Baptism, original sin, as well as the guilt
of sin actually committed, was taken away.
Hence, the practice soon became common of
delaying the reception of this grace, as long as
possible, lest after its reception, the person
should imperil his salvation by sinning, without
this means of getting rid of the penalty.

In most of the religions which preceded
Christianity there was a form of initiation very
similiar to that of Christian Baptism. In some
cases the rite was practically identical, and
those initiated were spoken of as regenerated, or
born again. In India, a missionary has to be
most careful to explain the Scriptural meaning
of the statement "ye must be born again," or his

hearers would imagine that he was teaching a familiar doctrine, very different in its significance from what was taught by our Lord. According to their belief, the members of the inferior castes must appear on earth as Bráhmans; then, and not until then, on their initiation into the mysteries they will be twice-born, and on the way to attain the supreme good;—absorption into the Divine Being from whom they came. In the old Chaldean mysteries, baptism was administered before instruction. In the rites of Isis and Mithra, baptism was practised; and, to the baptised, pardon and regeneration were promised. In the religion of our forefathers, and even in Mexico, a form of baptism was in use.

For the other things now added at the consecration of the water, Roman Catholic writers admit that they have no authority in Scripture. "We are not satisfied with that which the Apostles or Gospels do declare, but we say, that, as well before as after, there are divers matters of importance and weight accepted and received, out of a doctrine which is nowhere set forth in writing. For we do bless the water wherewith we baptize, and the oil wherewith we anoint; yes, and besides that, him that is christened. And out of what Scripture have we learned the same? Have we not it of a secret and unwritten ordinance? And further, what Scripture hath taught us to grease with oil? Yea, whence cometh it that we dip the child three times in the water?"[1] "And indeed Father Newman himself admits, in regard to Holy water and many other things that were, as he says, the 'very instruments and append-ages of demon worship' that they were all of pagan origin, and sanctified by adoption into the Church. What plea then, what palliation can be offered for so extraordinary adoption? Why this; that the Church 'had confidence in the power of Christianity to resist the infection of evil' and to transmute them to 'an evangelical use.'"[2]

It is painfully interesting to see how closely in some of these ceremonies connected with the consecration and use of holy water, the pagan copy has been followed. A lighted candle is put into the water, as a prayer is offered that

[1] Jodocus Tiletanus of Louvaine, quoted in *Two Babylons*, p. 199.

[2] *Ibid*, p. 230.

the Holy Ghost would enter, and give efficacy
to the water to wash away sin. What can be
the meaning of such an act? "The purifying
virtue of water, which, in pagan esteem, had
such efficacy in cleansing from sin, and regenerating the soul, was derived in part from the
passing of the mediatorial god, the sun god, the
god of fire, through these waters, during his
humiliation and sojourn in the midst of them."[1]
This deity was immersed in water, that he might
give efficacy to it, that when used for baptism
it might effect its great purpose of washing
away sin, and quickening the spiritual in those
who received it.   In the temples of Greece,
every person who came to the solemn sacrifice
was washed with water. To which end, at the
entrance of the temples there was commonly
placed a vessel full of holy water. This water
was consecrated by putting into it a burning
torch taken from the altar. The burning torch
was the express symbol of the god of fire. This
very same method is used in the Roman Church
for consecrating the water for baptism. The
unsuspicious testimony of Bishop Hay leaves

[1] *Two Babylons*, p. 207.

no doubt on this point. " It is blessed on the eve of Pentecost, because it is the Holy Ghost who gives to the waters of baptism, the power and efficacy of sanctifying our souls ; and because the baptism of Christ is with the Holy Ghost and with fire. In blessing the water a lighted torch is put into the font. Here then it is manifest that the baptismal regenerating water of Rome is consecrated just as the regenerating and purifying water of the Pagans was. Whilst the Romish doctrine in regard to baptism is purely pagan, in the ceremonies connected with the papal baptism, one of the essential rites of the ancient fire worship is still practised at this day."

In India, the belief in the soul-cleansing power of water is universal among the Hindus ; but as the climate is warm, the people immerse themselves in it rather than receive a sprinkling. Every stream is sacred, some are pre-eminently so. Those living near, bathe in them daily ; those whose home is at a distance visit them as pilgrims. Such is the efficacy of bathing, at certain places, on specially holy days, that by one act, all sin, past, present, and future, can be removed ; and the sins of the bathers' ancestors too. In the approach of death, if possible, the sick are removed to the banks of a sacred river, in the belief that the sight of the holy water will cleanse the soul, and afford a passport to heaven.

CHAPTER VII

TRANSUBSTANTIATION AND THE MASS.

IN the doctrine of transubstantiation, as taught in the Romish Church, it is affirmed that the wafer and wine used in the celebration of the Mass, up to a certain moment, are ordinary matter; by the act of consecration, *i.e.*, the repetition of the words "This is my body, this is my blood," this, though to outward appearance unchanged, is converted into the natural body and blood of our Lord. If this is true, it is the greatest miracle the world has ever heard of; if it be false, it is as great a fraud as the history of religion can show.

That this is a fair statement none can doubt, who read what Rome's Councils have decreed, and her accredited teachers have taught. Here are the words of the creed of Pope Pius IV., which was compiled as a summary of the decisions of the Council of Trent. " In the

most holy sacrament of the Eucharist there is
truly, really, and substantially, the Body and
Blood, together with the soul and divinity of our
Lord Jesus Christ; and there is a conversion of
the whole substance of the bread into the
Body, and of the whole substance of the wine
into the Blood, which conversion the Catholic
Church calls Transubstantiation." The Canons
of the Council on which this sentence is based are
the following: "If any shall say that He [*i.e.*,
Christ] is only in it [the Eucharist] as in a sign
or figure; that there remains the substance of
bread and wine along with the Body and Blood
of our Lord, although the appearance of bread
and wine remain; if any shall deny that,
in the sacrament of the Eucharist under each
kind [*i.e.* under the bread and wine], when a
separation is made, whole Christ is contained; if
any shall say that, when consecration has taken
place, the Body and Blood of our Lord is not
present, but is there only in use, while it is being
taken, but not before or after; and that in the
hosts, or consecrated particles which are reserved,
or remain after communion, there does not
remain the true Body of the Lord; and if any
say that in the sacrament of the Eucharist,

Christ is not to be adored with the worship of Latria [*i.e.* the worship due to God alone], nor to be publicly placed before the people in order to be adored, and that those who adore it are idolators, let him be accursed." In harmony with these Canons, the host is raised in the presence of the congregation to be adored ; part is reserved for administration to the sick ; and as it is carried through the streets at special festivals, the people are expected to bow their heads in worship.

What an awful perversion of a beautifully simple act of our Lord ! Reclining at the Passover feast, over which the head of the family usually presided, Jesus was surrounded by His chosen friends. The meal had been prepared with peculiar ceremonies to commemorate the deliverance God had wrought for His people on the eve of their departure from Egypt. Jesus took bread and wine remaining over from the feast, and, giving a little to each disciple, told them to continue the practice as a memorial of the great Sacrifice he had made, which would be completed, when, on the cross His body was broken, and blood shed. The Eucharist of the Romish Church differs in almost every particular from the instructions of the Saviour. In the upper room in Jerusalem it was celebrated at the close of a meal; now it must be taken fasting. There was no official priest necessary; now, only a priest can officiate. The disciples partook of the wine as well as of the bread; Rome restricts the use of the wine to the priests. And in order that the communicants may not regard this as a mutilated sacrament, a second miracle is said to be performed; the wafer which was changed into the body of our Lord, has then to be further changed into His blood. It is marvellous that such a perversion of our Lord's teaching could have been made; or that it can still be accepted. Dark indeed, were the centuries during which the change was effected. And, when light began to illuminate the Church, thousands of the best men and women were cruelly tortured and consigned to death because they raised their voice against this and other corruptions which had crept into the Church.

It is within comparatively recent times that this awful doctrine was taught in the form given above. In the Council of Trent the most diverse views were expressed by the recognised teachers of the Church. Many argued and voted against the view that was finally accepted. The Canons were carried by a small majority, composed largely of Italians, sent by the Pope, with the object of forcing his views upon the assembly. This servile set outnumbered by more than a hundred, the independent representatives of the rest of Christendom. Members of the minority openly expressed the opinion that it was useless to attempt to hold their ground against the Roman phalanx, who voted according to order rather than from conviction. Hitherto it had been an unwritten law of the Church, that practical unanimity was necessary before a decree could be made by a Council; on this fundamental question of the Eucharist, there was anything but practical unanimity.

The Council completed its work in 1570. In 1438, Cardinal Bessarion wrote as follows:

" Paul delivered to us that which he had received; but since he delivered that only which he writes in the Epistle to the Corinthians, that he alone received; and that alone saw the apostles do; for had he seen them do more, he would have delivered that also. And he, in that Epistle, says nothing more than that Christ broke bread

7

with His hands, blessed, and gave it to His
disciples and said, ' Take, eat, this is my body.'"
Some of the earlier writers refer to the Passion
ceremonies, and bear witness to the fact that
though Jesus *broke* the bread, this is not now-a-
days done in the services. In 1458, in a discussion between a Jew and a Christian, the way
in which the disciples present at the inauguration
of the feast would understand their Master's
words is well brought out. " As Christ said ' This
is my body,' so we in like manner say ' This is
the bread which our fathers ate in the land of
Egypt, though that bread has long since passed
away and exists no more. Thus it is sufficient
for Christians to say, that the sacrifice of the
altar is in memory of that bread of Christ,
though this bread is not that." [1]

When the early Christians were taunted by
the heathen that they had no sacrifices in their
churches, they replied that they offered to God
what was better than a sacrifice of material
things :—faith, love, obedience. This is a very
different reply from what would be given by the
modern Romanist.

[1] *Romanism*, p. 126.

The Canon of the Mass is quite opposed to what is taught in the Creed of Pius IV. When that was written very different views were held from those which prevailed in later years. This was clearly noticed by Bossuet, who undertook to write a work for the benefit of those who, by fear of persecution, had been driven into the churches of his diocese. But the difficulties he attempted to clear away still remain. The Canon of the Mass and the decisions of the Council of Trent, as condensed in the Pope's creed, are in absolute contradiction.

1. " The only oblation recognised in the Canon of the Mass is the offering of alms, of first-fruits, and of the elements intended for consecration ; the oblation thus preceding the consecration.

2. " The idea of a corporal presence in the Eucharist was then absolutely unknown, and, had it been known, would have been eagerly repudiated.

3. " The service implies throughout the communication of all present.

4. " Who all communicate in both kinds, as is admitted even by the Roman advocates them-

selves thus leaving no distinctive participation for the priest alone." [1]

Such was the custom prior to the 16th century. From the words of the more ancient liturgy then in use, the Mass consisted of three parts; an oblation or gift to God of bread and wine as an expression of thanks for His goodness; the consecration of these gifts into memorials of Jesus Christ; and finally, the reception of these by the believers, who, by this means, were rendered an acceptable sacrifice to God.

As a specimen of the views held at the Council of Trent, the following are given. Cardinal Cajetan thus expresses what he conceived to be the teaching of the Scriptures. Writing a comment on Hebrews x. 18, "now where remission of sin is, there is no more offering for sin," he says, " From the fact that by the new law remission of sins is made by the one offering of Christ, no other offering for sin remains. For, in such a case, an injury would be done to the offering of Christ, as though it were insufficient. Nor let the novice on this account be surprised that the sacrifice of the altar be duly offered in the

[1] *Romanism*, p. 132.

Church of Christ. For this is not a new sacrifice, but a commemoration of that which Christ offered, according to Christ's own charge, 'This do ye in remembrance of me.' For all the sacraments of Christ are nothing less than the application of the passion of Christ to the receivers. It is one thing, however, to repeat the passion of Christ, and another to repeat the commemoration and application of His passion." [1]

Cardinal Contarini says practically the same. " Do we not in the Canon say ' Receive, O Holy Trinity, this oblation which we offer to Thee in remembrance of the passion of our Lord Jesus Christ ? ' and ' This do in remembrance of Me ? ' It is expressly said that we make a remembrance of the passion of Christ, by which one sacrifice we are reconciled to God." [2] This is the very opposite to the statement in the creed, viz., that " in the Mass there is offered to God a true, proper and propiatory sacrifice for the living and the dead." In another book he says " in what manner is the Mass a sacrifice ? It is a sacrifice of praise, it is a sacrifice of thanksgiving, it is a

[1] *Romanism*, p. 137.

[2] *Ibid*, p. 138.

sacrifice because it is the memory of that only sacrifice by which Christ through the Holy Ghost offered Himself up for us to the Father."

There were four distinct views held then on this important question. " Some affirmed that Christ offered Himself in the supper, and, therefore it was propiatory sacrifice. The second view was that the sacrifice was not propiatory but a sacrifice of thanksgiving. The third was that Christ offered Himself simply, and not in a propiatory manner. And lastly there was the opinion adopted and represented in the canons of the Council."[1] By the Italian contingent this was forced on the Council, although it was admitted that it was not capable of proof from Scriptures, and was opposed to the common faith of the teachers of the Church.

It is strange that any sane man can believe, or any good man teach, that it is possible to eat his God. And yet this is what this doctrine of transubstantiation comes to. We have given reasons for believing that many doctrines and ceremonies distinctive of the Roman Catholic Church have their origin in heathenism. But

[1] *Romanism*, p. 139.

this goes beyond the doctrines of paganism. "When we call fruit Ceres," writes Cicero, "and wine Bacchus we employ a common usage of language. But who, think you, would be so mad as to believe that that which we have eaten is a deity?" "Since these Christians," exclaimed the philosopher Averroes on his deathbed, "devour the God they worship, let my soul be with the philosophers."[1] And this is not an unfair statement of our apponets' views. Here is the teaching of S. Alphonsus Ligouri, in his well known work entitled, "Visits to the Blessed Sacrament," a devotional book recognised as suitable reading for the faithful. "St. Paul extols the obedience of Jesus Christ by telling us that He obeyed His eternal Father unto death. But in this Sacrament His obedience is still more wonderful, since He is pleased not only to obey His eternal Father, but even man himself. Yes the King of Heaven descends from His throne in obedience to the voice of man, and remains upon our altars, according to His pleasure. He is there without motion, or apparent will, suffering Himself to

[1] *Romanism*, p. 141.

be carried about from place to place, and to be given in communion, both to the just and to sinners. Whilst He lived on earth He was obedient to His blessed mother and St. Joseph ; but in this Sacrament He obeys as many creatures as there are priests upon earth."[1]

It is not surprising that the Romish Church should teach in the Catechism of the Council of Trent, that " Since Bishops and Priests as the interpreters of God, are both a kind of mediators, who in His name teach men the Divine Law, and the precepts of life, and sustain the part of God Himself on earth, it is plain that no greater function can be imagined than theirs ; wherefore they are deservedly called not only angels, but even Gods, since they have, among us, the power and the divinity of the immortal God."[2]   And further, it is affirmed that the priests of the New Testament far exceed all others in honour.   For the power which is conferred upon them of making, as well the Body and Blood of our Lord, and of remitting

[1] *English Edition of Works*, p. 70.   Quoted in *Primer of Rom. Cath.*, p. 54

[2] *Primer of Roman Catholicism*, p. 78.

sins, surpasses human reason and intelligence, nor can anything equal or like to it be found on earth."[1] Something like, though not equal to it, is, as we shall see, common in Hinduism, and in other heathen systems.

The blasphemy of this teaching is appaling. In Butler's *Lives of the Saints* it is affirmed that "the Eucharist is offered as a perpetual sacrifice, by which our sin might be expiated, and our heavenly Father be won from wrath to mercy."

It was in the year 1215 that the doctrine of the corporal presence of Christ in the Eucharist was forced upon the Church by Innocent III. But owing to the opposition which his teaching aroused, he modified his views, so as to limit the period of the change in the bread and wine to the moment they were taken into the mouth. This modified view was condemned by the Council of Trent.

The doctrine of the transforming of wafer and wine into the actual body and blood of our Lord is supported by legends of miracles wrought to confirm the faith of the doubtful. " A priest

[1] *Primer of Roman Catholicism*, 79.

implored the Almighty to let him see and
handle Christ present in the Holy Eucharist.
His prayer was granted ; he saw upon the altar
the infant Christ. He was bidden by an angel
to take the Child in his arms. He did so,
fondly embraced Him and kissed His eyes.
He then replaced Him upon the Altar, and
implored the Lord to assume His former shape.
The prayer was answered, and the Child was
again transformed into the ordinary Host.
Saints are reported to have seen the elevated
Host presenting the appearance of a boy,
shining like the sun, expressing approbation
with His looks, and speaking with His tongue,
and going into the mouths of communicants
when they were receiving the Eucharist."   In
pictures, as in words, this fiction of a perverted
imagination is represented so as to appeal to the
mind through the eyes of the most ignorant.   A
figure of the Saviour is represented as rising
from the wafer when raised for adoration.   Pope
Gregory VII. is said to have authorized a vigil
in the Church of S. Anastasia in Rome in order
that a miracle might occur, similar to one which

occurred in the time of Gregory the Great; that a finger might be seen in the place of the wafer. The vigil was kept, but the narrator confesses that the sign desired was not forthcoming. The manufacture of legends of miracles to confirm the faith of the doubter is not peculiar to the Papal Church. In India, similar stories are found in abundance so that it is difficult to accept as trustworthy, accounts of miracles wrought in support of doctrines, or to lead to the performance of special religious ceremonies.

The objection raised by the senses to the fact of any change in the wafer and wine on the altar, is skilfully anticipated in the Catechism of the Council of Trent. Seeing that the wafer may become corrupt, and the wine sour, even after the stupendous miracle has been wrought on it, how can it be ascertained that the transformation has been affected? "Since by the common nature of men, it is abhorrent to be fed with human flesh and blood, He most wisely caused that the most holy body and blood should be ministered to us under the appearance of those things, namely, bread and wine, by the daily and common sustenance of which we are specially gratified. And, moreover, there are combined these two advantages : we are saved from the calumnies of the infidels, which we could not avoid, if we were seen to eat our Lord under his proper appearance ; and, while we partake of the body and blood of our Lord in such a manner, that, though truly, it cannot be perceived by the senses, this is of the greatest efficacy in increasing faith in our souls."[1]

In order to true consecration, pure wheat must be used for the wafer, and the wine must be pure juice of the grape. And further, there must be a definite intention on the part of the celebrant to consecrate all the elements he has prepared. If the officiating priests, from any cause, fail to have this definite intention, no change is effected, and the unconsecrated host being elevated, the people are guilty of idolatry ; they give to wafer and wine the adoration which can rightly be given to God alone.

When Jesus instituted this Sacrament, He took the bread remaining over from the Passover Feast, and brake it, and gave it to His disciples. In place of bread, a round, flat wafer has been

[1] *Primer of Catholicism*, p. 51.

substituted, called a host. This was the word usually employed in pagan Rome for the sacrificial victims offered on their altars. As far as is known, the wafer was first used by Christian converts in Arabia, where they had been used as offerings to the local deities. The use of them was forbidden in the Church as associated with heathenism ; but afterwards the prohibition was removed, and their use became common in the Western Church. In the Eastern Church ordinary bread is still used.

In another respect, the example of our Lord is disregarded ; the wine is withheld from the people, the wafer only given. The first indication of this practice is found in the thirteenth century. There was considerable objection raised to the innovation, the people imagining that they were defrauded of a right. But the Church affirmed that under either bread or wine, "a whole and entire Christ, and a true sacrament was received." Yet, strange to say, in the recorded visions by which the faith of the people in this doctrine is confirmed, part only of the body of our Lord was said to have been seen. The reasons for this practice are as follows :— to avoid spilling a drop of the blood of Jesus on the ground; the Eucharist ought always to be available for the dying; if the wine be kept too long, it may become sour; wine of the right kind cannot always easily be obtained: to refute the heresy of those who asserted that a bloodless sacrifice was under the appearance of the bread. In some countries the withholding of the wine from the people led to serious riots, and the old order was temporarily restored until the pre-judices of the people were overcome.

Such is Romanism. In India there is a striking analogy in the consecration of their images. On days, sacred to a deity, temporary images are provided for use at the festival. These are made of mud from a sacred stream. While in the hands of the workman, they possess no sacred character. When finished they are taken to the house where the ceremony is to be held, and up to a certain moment are regarded as gaily decorated lumps of mud. On the eve of the festival, the act of life-giving is performed. A priest recites texts, by which an invitation is given to the deity to visit the house and inhabit the image as his temporary dwelling. The eyes, nose, ears, mouth, hands, feet of the idol are touched in turn, by which, and the repetition of special texts, a notable miracle has been wrought; the image is now supposed to be a living god. Only Brahmans may approach it; and their services are necessary to present the gifts that the family wish to offer. When the worship is over, a reverse process is gone through. The deity is thanked for his presence, and dismissed, and the image is thrown into the river from which it came. The noticeable feature of the transaction is: that by the repetition of a formula, and the performance of certain ritual, the mud is made divine and becomes a proper object of adoration. Legends are not lacking to show how want of faith in the supposed miracle has been punished. Some are said to have been struck blind, others killed for presuming to treat the image as though it were not divine.

Where is there the slightest authority in the Scriptures for the belief that a priest can perform the greatest miracle the world has ever witnessed;—convert bread and wine into a God, and demand the adoration of the faithful. If there is a whole Christ in any particle, how many are there in a whole wafer? Though God is omnipresent, what evidence is there that the human body of Jesus Christ has the power of

infinite extension ?   There was no manifestation
of this when he was on earth amongst men ;
rather the opposite.   If the subject were not so
sacred, it furnishes abundant matter for ridicule.
And yet this has been and still is the teaching
of a Church which professes to be infallible !

CHAPTER VIII

THE FATHER FORGOTTEN; THE SAINTS ADORED

In Roman Catholic communities, by many people, the direct worship of God has practically ceased; the altars where the Saviour is represented are largely neglected, whilst those of the Virgin Mary and the saints attract the majority of the worshippers. The explanation is simple. Being afraid of the infinitely merciful Father they hope to secure His favour through the powerful intercession of these venerated persons, and hence direct to them the adoration due to God alone.

India furnishes an analogous case. The Hindus affirm that "God is one without a second," and in the same breath, with equal emphasis, add that the One has manifested himself in millions of forms. Very probably this declaration of the divine unity is a survival from the faith of their ancestors. The farther back

8

their religious history is traced, the fewer are their objects of worship, and there seems good reason for believing that at one time monotheism prevailed. But now all this is changed. The One, who except by the more thoughtful is practically forgotten, has manifested himself in three chief forms, called the Creator, the Preserver, and the Destroyer. Of these, the Creator is largely ignored; having finished the work of creation, he has nothing more to give his worshippers. But as the Preserver and the Destroyer are still influential, their aid is sought, with costly gifts, or physical suffering. At various times, and in various forms, it is affirmed they have appeared on earth, and, with their wives, attract the adoration of the people. The supreme has been supplanted by the three; and, these again, have been supplanted by later, so-called incarnations.

In addition to these divine beings, saints and heroes have been raised to the position of demigods, to whom worship is rendered, identical with that which is given to the gods themselves. And this is justified on the ground that their intercession will be helpful. Afraid to go direct to a divine being, they try to interest these friends at court on their behalf.

The teaching of the Church of Rome is almost identical with this. "The saints, reigning together with Christ, offer to God, their prayers for men; and it is good and useful to invoke them with supplications; but they who deny that they, enjoying eternal happiness in heaven, are to be invoked; or who assert that they do not pray for men, or that the invoking them is idolatry, or that it is contrary to the word of God, and opposed to the honour of the one Mediator between God and man, or that it is folly, either by word or thought to supplicate them are impious in their opinions."

Is it surprising, that, thus instructed, the people should pray to and worship human beings who have passed away? It is true that in the Romish Church it is affirmed that worship is of three kinds;—the lowest such as can rightly be given to saints and angels; a higher appropriately offered to the Virgin Mary; the highest to God alone. But who can distinguish these? If the essence of idolatry is to give to a creature, what is due to the Creator only, how dangerous, to use no stronger terms, is it to teach that worship of any kind can rightly be offered save to God Himself. Roman Catholics have freely admitted this.   At first many of her teachers deemed it unwise to allow the practice of invoking the saints, lest their converts should retain their old superstitions.

What is the natural consequence of this teaching?   Sinful people find it easier to repair to their fellow men for sympathy and help than to the great God and Father; or to the mighty Saviour.   In the Cathedral at Canterbury was a shrine of Jesus Christ, another of the Virgin, and another of Thomas-a-Becket.   In the boxes, placed to receive the offerings of those who sought the intercession of these advocates, on a certain day, St. Thomas' box contained £100; the Virgin's, £10, that before the Saviour was empty!   Whilst many invoked the help of a man, none sought that of the Divine.

In an illustrated edition of the life of St. Francis, published by authority, are two instructive pictures.   In one the Saviour is represented as sitting in His throne judging the world.   The Virgin, seated at His feet, is asking Him to spare it, and, in answer to her prayer He does so.   In the other, the saint is seen dragging souls out of the scorching flames of Purgatory.

Conversing with a lady educated in a convent, it seemed to her as a real revelation, that God was gracious ; more ready to bless than His children to pray. It was an axiomatic truth with her up to that time, that without the aid of powerful intercessors it was vain to ask His favour.

In praying to saints, a very important matter seems to be overlooked. A man may reasonably ask counsel and help from a friend in matters spiritual and secular, provided that friend is at hand, and able to assist. Or, if he be at a distance, a letter may be sent to him. But what proof, what hint have we in the Scriptures, that the saints, finite in knowledge, and unable, when here, to be in more than one place at a time, have become omniscient so as to hear the prayers of thousands of people, and omnipresent, so as to be able to assist their numerous suppliants ? In life their knowledge and power were limited, what evidence have we that death has endowed them with divine attributes to enable them to know the wants of all who pray to them. If there were no harm in worshipping them, how can they be conscious of the adoration of many men in many places.

In his history of the Christian Church, Milman says, " Men passed from rational respect for the remains of the dead, the communion of holy thought and emotion which might connect the departed saint with his brethren in the flesh, to the superstitious veneration of relics, and the deification of mortal men, by so easy a transition, that they never discovered the precise point at which they transgressed the unmarked, and unwatched boundary. The worshipper felt and acknowledged his dependence on these intermediate beings, the intercessors with the intercessor. They were arrayed, by the general belief, in some of the attributes of Deity— ubiquity; the perpetual cognizance of the affairs of the earth ; they could hear prayer, they could read the heart, they could control nature ; they had a power derivative, aided from a higher source, but still exercised according to their volition over all the events of the world. Thus each city, and almost each individual began to have his tutelar saint; the presence of some beatified being hovered over and hallowed particular spots, and thus the strong influence of local and particular worships combined again with that great universal faith of which the great Father was the sole object, and the universe, the temple.[1] And He expresses the opinion that the Christians believed as firmly in the existence of the old pagan deities as the people who continued to worship them ; hence their fierceness in demolishing the temples and casting down the idols.[2]

" An illustration of the new form assumed by Christian worship may be seen in Paulinus, who celebrates the nativity of St. Felix, the tutelary saint of Nola. St Felix is at least invested with the power ascribed to the intermediate deities of antiquity. Pilgrims crowded from the whole of south Italy to his festival. Rome, though she possessed the altars of St. Peter and Paul, poured forth myriads. St. Felix is implored by his servants to remove the impediments to their pilgrimage from the hostility of men and adverse weather, to smooth the seas, and send prosperous winds. There is a constant reference indeed to Christ as the source of his power, yet the power is fully and explicity assigned to the saint. He is the prevailing intercessor between

[1] *History of Christianity*, v. iii., p. 543.

[2]   Do   p. 144.

the worshipper and Christ. But the vital distinctions between the paganised form of Christianity itself is no less manifest in the poems. It is not merely as a tutelary deity in this life that the saint is invoked ; the future state of existence, the final judgment are constantly present to the thought of the worshippers. St. Felix is entreated after death, to bear the souls of his worshippers into the bosom of the Redeemer, and to intercede for them at the last day."[1]

Christianity spread rapidly in the towns, be cause the teachers could readily reach the people there ; and because the reforming arm of the law enforced the new regulations. Hence the term pagan, meaning one who dwelt in the country, became a synonym for one who followed old religious cults. But such was the ignorance of many of those country converts, that they trembled lest the forsaken deities might punish them for their infidelity and neglect. It is therefore highly probable that it was not until the whole of the tutelary deities had been replaced by what may justly be called the inferior deities of paganized Christianity, saints, martyrs

[1] Millman's *History of Christianity*, v. iii., p. 543.

and angels, that Christianity was extensively
or permanently established in the rural districts.
To these saints of the new religion, distinct
duties were assigned as was commonly the case
with the gods of the old.   Thus St. Cecilia is the
patron of musicians, St. Luke of artists, St. Peter
of fishmongers, and St. Crispus of cobblers.   St.
Theodorus takes the place of Romulus, and is
supposed to heal the sick, and SS. Cosmos
and Damianus are the successors of Æsculapius.
These were martyrs in Ægæan Cilicia where
the god of health was commonly worshipped.
Years after their death, they are said to have
appeared to the Emperor Justinian in Byzantium,
and their worship, especially among the sick,
spread far and wide. [1]

The number of saints to whom prayers can
be addressed is increased from time to time.
At first bishops had the power to canonize any
whom they considered worthy of the honour,
but since the 12th century the prerogative has
been vested in the Pope.   An imposing service is
held at which the process of saint making is
performed.   The names of the illustrious dead

---

[1] Taylor's *Primitive Culture*, p. 47.

are proposed, and their virtues eloquently ex-
tolled ; proofs are given of miracles performed
by them after their decease; whilst an ecclesiastic
styled " the devil's advocate " raises objections to
the canonization. If the objections are considered valid, the honour is refused; if his
charges are declared non-proven, or trivial, the
addition to the goodly array of saints is completed. The list is lengthy and goes back into
the early ages of the world. There are more
than enough for every day of the year to be
honoured with one, so those who cannot have a
day for themselves share one with others, and
that none may be omitted, they are honoured en
masse on all saints' day.

Who are the men and women who have
received this signal mark of honour, whose intercession, it is affirmed, is a Christian's duty to
invoke? Noah is worthy of considerable respect,
seeing that faithful amongst the faithless, he
believed in God, and amid the ridicule of his
neighbours obeyed His command. But who
would think of invoking his aid? Yet in 1855
the Archbishop of Florentine thought differently.
For years the grape vintage in Tuscany had
failed, and in order to bring about a better state

of affairs, he published eight prayers for help in this matter, one of which is addressed to Noah. Presumably, as the patriarch had successfully passed through a flood, he could assist those undergoing a similar affliction. One passage is very striking. "Most Holy Patriarch, Noah! who didst employ thyself in thy long career in cultivating the vine, and gratifying the human race with that precious beverage which allays the thrist, restores the strength, and enlivens the spirit of us all : deign to regard our vines, which, following thine example, we have cultured hitherto, and, when thou beholdest them languishing and blighted by that disastrous visitation which before the vintage, destroys the fruit (in severe punishment for many blasphemies and other enormous sins we have committed) have compassion on us, and, prostrate before the lofty throne of God, who has promised to His children the fruits of the earth, and abundance of corn and wine, entreat Him on our behalf; promise Him, in our name, that with the aid of divine grace, we will forsake the ways of vice and sin, that we will no longer abuse his sacred gifts, and will scrupulously observe His holy law, and that of our holy Mother, the Catholic Church," etc. This collection of

prayers concludes with one to the Virgin Mary
in which the phraseology differs from that used
in invoking Noah.   She is implored herself to
save the vines from destruction; Noah is asked
to implore God to grant their protection.

The great company of saints, who, by canonization have been made into a spiritual aristocracy,
contains some worthy of the respect of the whole
world, some who were not conspicuous for goodness, and some who were positively bad.   Some
lived before the Christian age, and never heard
of many doctrines, for the non acceptance of
which men are pronounced accursed; others,
since that age, who in important questions such
as the Supremacy of the Pope, the invocation of
Saints, the existence of Purgatory, have openly
expressed opinions opposed to those authoritatively taught; and yet others, who, though
guilty of grave crimes, were useful members of
the one true Church.   How some of these can
be regarded as helpful to the tried and tempted
is difficult to see.   And as some were canonized
by men who were usurpers of the Papal throne,
their title to sainthood must be a doubtful one.

The practice of raising the spirits of the departed
into demi-gods was frequent in Europe before the

Christian age. Whilst the greater gods were common to Rome and other nations, each district had its own local deities. To these were added the manes, or spirits of their ancestors. Later on came the deification of the Emperors, both dead and living. When, therefore, people familiar with the idea of mortals being raised to the position of gods, came into the Church, they wanted some inferior deities to take the place of those they were commanded to forsake. These people lived in fear of the infinitely great and merciful Father, and sought the aid of those who had passed into His presence as intercessors. Their teachers, therefore, provided them with saints and martyrs, who, in time, came to be regarded as demi-gods, only slightly inferior to the Virgin and her divine Son. The process was a somewhat lengthy one by which a favour was obtained—a saint was besought to intercede with the Virgin, who, in her turn, would intercede with the Saviour, and He would use His influence with the Father. Strange indeed that this could be possible when Jesus had declared that as the Father loved His children, knowing their wants, He would give all necessary good, even without His own pleading on behalf of suppliants.

To a Protestant it seems strange that people
can believe in the existence of a great number
of gods ; but a little thought will show that it is
not unnatural. The universe is vast, the wants
of men are many. As under an Emperor are
subordinate officers, each having charge of a
department, so they imagine it to be in God's
government. They think that He is too great
to attend to the trivial affairs of mortals, and has
delegated His power of control to subordinates.
Hence, it is believed, that there are gods of the
heavens, gods of the earth, gods of the sea, and
gods of the rivers. And the custom is, for a
suppliant to seek the help of the one in charge
of a department, rather than of the Supreme.
The newly converted heathen crowded into the
Church, with their minds filled with these superstitions, and saints and angels were provided to
take the place of these deities to whom they had
been accustomed to pray. It is true, that in the
Church formularies, the worship which is given
to saints is said to be inferior in kind to that
which is given to God. Yet it is undoubtedly
true that the ignorant Christian, as the ignorant
pagan, lavishes his devotion on the inferior
being, who, as he believes, has given directly, or

obtained by his intercession, the desired boon. God alone can pardon, says the formulary ; but to whom is the gratitude of the pardoned soul given? God alone can heal ; but the votive offering is laid at the foot of the image of the Virgin Mary.

If further proof were wanted that Christian saints occupy the place once given to pagan deities, we have it in the fact that hills, springs, and other places of resort, once known by the name of the old gods, now have Christian names ; and the special benefits obtained at these places are sought from their modern guardians. The following hymn addressed to St. Rosolia, the protectress of Palermo, is almost identical in spirit with what was commonly sung to heathen guardians of cities :—

> "Virgin modest as the rose,
> Fairer than the lily's snows ,
> Listen, whilst our lips disclose
> A nations prayer—
> Nature's scourges banish hence,
> Earthquake, battle, pestilence ;
> Oh grant us but thy firm defence
> And come what dare."[1]

[1] Blunt's *Vestiges*, p. 19.

Blunt gives the following account of the way in which Christians have substituted saints for the old pagan deities.

They are the Lares, or household gods, and are placed at the meetings of roads as of old, and are decorated with flowers and corn. They are made guardians of homes; niches at the entrance being occupied by images of the Virgin and saints. They have places in the rooms, where they are represented by image or picture, and frequently a lamp burns in front of them. They are guardians of the bed; they are protectors of travellers by land and sea. They give names to vessels, as was common with the old deities. Their figures are worn as charms; and, as of old, were statues of the gods in the fields as guardians and protectors, some crucifixes and images of the saints occupy their old places.[1] In the Cathedral of Lucca is an altar with the inscription, " Christo liberatori ac Deis Tutelarilus." To Christ, the Deliverer, and to the Guardian Deities." The very word being used for the guardian saints which was usually employed by the pagan Roman for his guardian gods!

---

[1] Blunt's *Vestiges* p, 20, ff.

Not only have the old statues of pagan deities been utilized as the representatives of Christian saints, but old legends, concerning some of the better known, have been copied or adapted to give peculiar glory to similar ones now in use· Tacitus tells a story of the introduction of the image of Serapis into Alexandria. Ptolemy had sent to Pontus for this popular image, but king and people objected to its removal. So it is said that it quietly walked on board a ship, and in due time reached Alexandria, where a magnificent temple was erected to receive it. At Lucca is a celebrated image of the Saviour, called the Volto Santo. This, according to the legend, was made in Palestine, but as the workman engaged could not form a suitable head, one came direct from heaven. A Piedmontese Bishop was anxious to secure this wonderful work. Seeing a vessel in the port of Joppa, without anyone on board, the Bishop, carrying his treasure, reached the ship, and as soon as he stepped on deck, the vessel started and sailed to Lerici without captain and men. On reaching port, no one but the Bishop was able to lift the image, but he carried it to Lucca, where it has since remained.

9

As an illustration of the attitude of ignorant people towards certain saints it is affirmed that recently an old woman was heard praying in a Church. She asked God to *beseech* St. Anthony of Padua to find her keys for her !

CHAPTER IX

MARIOLATRY

IN the previous chapter, it has been indicated, how, in the Christian Church, saints have been raised to the position once occupied by the inferior deities of paganism; in this chapter attention is called to the worship of the Virgin Mary.

Two circumstances may be regarded as the chief factors in originating her worship. Very early in the history of the Church, controversies of the fiercest character were carried on concerning the person of Christ. In the heat of discussion those who differed in opinion were vigorously cursed by their opponents, and consigned to the fires of hell. The name of the loving Jesus thus became intimately associated with what was fierce and fearful, and men fancied that some one more tender and gracious was needed to render their approach to God less

terrible.   Who so suitable as His mother?
Would not she, who procured by her intercession,
wine for the wedding guests at Cana, plead for
the sinful and sorrowful.

Another, and, in the case of many, still more
powerful reason, was this.   In their pagan days
they had worshipped goddesses as well as gods.
Whilst Jupiter and his male associates had been
clothed with the sterner and more dreadful
attributes of Deity, the goddesses were the
impersonations of the more gentle and loveable.
The early Christians missed this class of divinity.
Accordingly Mary was gradually raised from
her humble position.   Succeeding generations of
preachers and writers surpassed their predecessors
in sounding her praise, until she has come to be
regarded practically as divine, to whom worship,
second only to that which is due to God Himself,
can be rightly offered.   And her grace has been
so lavishly sung, that many approach her with
greater confidence of being heard than when
they direct their appeal to the All-merciful
Father, and His All-gracious Son.

That in thus speaking there is no exaggeration, the following extracts from Rome's accredited
teachers clearly prove.   The Council of Trent

did not in its Canons authorize the worship of the Virgin, but in the Catechism based upon its decrees are these words: "rightly has the Holy Church of Christ joined to this, giving of thanks, prayers and supplications to the most Holy mother of God, by which, suppliantly, we might fly to her, that she would, by her intercession, reconcile God to us sinners, and obtain for us those good things which are necessary for us to this life and to life eternal."[1]

"We have to go a long way back in the history of the Church before we reach the commencement of this practice. In the 4th century when the Council of Nice was called to condemn the heresy of Arius concerning the person of Christ, in order to secure a majority on the orthodox side, Bishops from Egypt were summoned. According to their belief, the three persons forming the Trinity were, 'The Father, the Virgin Mary, and the Messiah,' and Dr. Newman, referring to this astounding fact, elicited by the Nicene Council, speaks of these discussions as tending to the glorification of Mary. 'Thus the controversy opened a question

---

[1] *Tract*, by Rev. Prebendary Pennington, p. 11.

which it did not settle. It discovered a new
sphere, if we may so speak, in the realms of light
to which the Church had not yet assigned an
inhabitant. Thus there was a wonder in heaven ;
a throne was seen far above all created powers,
mediatorial, intercessary, a title archetypal, a
crown bright as the morning star, a glory issuing
from the eternal throne ; robes pure as the
heavens, and a sceptre over all, and who was the
predestined heir of that majesty ? Who was
that wisdom, and what was her name, the mother
of fair love, and fear, and holy hope, exalted like
a palm tree in Engadi, and a rose plant of
Jericho, created from the beginning, before the
world, in God's counsels, and in Jerusalem
was her power? The vision is found in the
Apocalypse, a woman clothed with the sun, and
the moon under her feet, and upon her head a
crown of twelve stars. The votaries of Mary do
not exceed the true faith, unless the blasphemers
of her Son come up to it. The Church of
Rome is not idolarous, unless Arianism is
orthodoxy.'[1] Such is the language of an English
divine in the nineteenth century. If Jesus is

[1] *Two Babylons*, p. 119.

divine, and not as Arius taught, a created and therefore subordinate being, then Mary is to be exalted and worshipped. If she holds a 'sceptre over all' surely she can be little, if at all, less than God. And this is acknowledged in some quarters, for in Lisbon is a Church with this inscription, "To the Virgin *goddess* of Loretto, the Italian race devoted to her *divinity*, have dedicated this temple."

Such a confession would probably be repudiated by many, who do not, however, shrink from giving her the intermediate homage which is declared lawful. But from what follows, evidently there is scarcely an appreciable difference in the attitude of the soul towards her from what is proper to God only.

In what is known as the Liturgy of St. James, which, though bearing the honoured name of an apostle, in its present form was unknown to him, we find these words addressed to the Virgin Mary. "Oh, Mother of ineffable light, honouring thee with angelic songs, we exalt, we magnify thy name. It is meet and just that we pronounce thee truly blessed, Mother of God, ever blessed, and in all the ways of thy life, unblameable and pure! Mother of our God, in dignity and honour above the cherubim, and in glory above the seraphim, thou, who, without spot or stain of human corruption, didst bring forth God the Word, thee truly do we exalt and magnify! To thee, O full of grace, every created being pours forth its congratulations. To thee who art the hallowed temple, the spiritual paradise from whom God assumed flesh and became a child ; the God who is before all ages! Truly did He make thy womb a throne that heaven itself could not surpass in glory! Thou who didst bring forth the true God, pray to Him, O Virgin, on our behalf, that He would bless and save our souls."

The phrase "Mother of God" here twice repeated, and now commonly employed in addresses to the Virgin, was not admitted into the Church without protest. It came into use, possibly through the action of converts in Africa who transferred the worship, formerly paid to Venus, to the mother of our Lord, in which they retained some familiar pagan ceremonies. In the fifth century Anastatius, a presbyter, preached against its use, and in this was supported by Nestorius, Bishop of Constantinople. But the Council of Ephesus adopted it, and since then it has been regarded as proper. Now the epithet, Mater Dei, Mother of God, was a name of Cybele, a very popular goddess in Italy. And proof that the worship of this pagan deity has been transformed to the Virgin, is seen in the fact that Lady Day, now devoted especially to her worship, formerly was Cybele's great festival.

In "The Garden of the Soul," a well-known devotional work, are the following, amongst many other epithets, equally striking :—" Holy Mother of God," " Mother of divine grace," "Gate of heaven," Morning star," " Refuge of sinners," " Comforter of the afflicted." It will be noticed that some of these are, in the Scripture, applied to Jesus Christ, and the Holy Spirit. And in harmony with such phrases is the following prayer :—" Oh, Holy Mother of God, despise not our petitions but obtain our deliverance in all dangers. Pray for us that we may be made worthy of the promise of Christ."

Another work entitled " The Glories of Mary," by Liguori, a saint canonized in 1839, carries the instruction farther still. " Although Mary is under an infinite obligation to her Son, for having chosen her to be His mother, it cannot

be denied, but that the son is under great obligation to her for having given Him His humanity ;
and therefore honours her in an especial manner
by granting all her petitions." But this is surpassed in an awful travesty of one of the grand-
est texts in the Bible, given as a quotation from
Bonaventura ; " As it is written of the love of
the Eternal Father that ' He so loved the world
as to give his only begotten son,' so also we can
say of Mary, that ' she so loved the world as to
give her only begotten Son for us.' " In a
similar spirit, with varied phraseology, this teaching is reiterated through the book. " The way
of salvation is open to none, otherwise than
through Mary." " Whoever expects to obtain
graces without the intercession of Mary, endeav-
ours to fly without wings." " Go to Mary, for
God has decreed that he will grant no grace
otherwise than by the hand of Mary." "All
power is granted to thee [Mary] in heaven and
on earth, and nothing is impossible to thee."
" God has placed the whole Church under the
dominion of Mary." " To become the mother
of God, the Blessed Virgin had to be raised to
a sort of equality with the Divine Persons, by
an almost infinity of graces." In a professed

quotation from another writer he says " You, oh Holy Virgin, have over God the authority of a mother, and hence can obtain pardon for the most obdurate of sinners." And in another, " You, oh Holy Virgin, can effect by your prayers all that God can operate by His power."

Not only in phrases which might be regarded as the impassioned utterances of an excited imagination is the adoration of the Virgin encouraged. Stories easily understood and re-membered are told to show that it is both easier and safer to go for salvation to Mary than to her divine Son. " Brother Leo saw a red ladder on the summit of which was Jesus Christ, and a white one on the top of which was His holy mother. Some who tried again and again to ascend the red ladder fell back ; they then tried the white one and easily ascended it, for our Blessed Lady stretched forth her hand to help them and they got safely into heaven. Mary is the mistress of heaven, for there she commands as she wills, and admits as she wills." [1] In other devotional works, though the form of words is different, the teaching is practically the same.

[1] *Primer of Roman Catholicism*, p. 124.

One writer declares that Mary was the repairer of the guilt of Eve as our Lord was of that of Adam." And another, Professor Oswald, affirms that " She was the Woman as Christ was the Man, and that she is co-present in the Eucharist, and that it is an indisputable fact, according to the Eucharistic doctrine of the Church, this presence of Mary is true and real, not merely ideal or figurative."[1] In the decree concerning the Immaculate Conception, which was authoritatively declared in 1854, Pope Pius IX. declared that she " rose from the dead, and being assumed on high, became Queen of heaven." In a picture of the crucifixion, Mary is represented with a sword through her breast; at the foot this explanation is given :—" Thy beloved Son did sacrifice His flesh, thou thy soul; yea, thy soul and body." With such teaching how is it possible for the people to restrict their worship to what, according to the formularies of the Church, is due to the Virgin ?

Where such views are held of her powerful influence it is not to be wondered at that in seasons of danger her aid has been sought, and

[1] *The Two Babylons*, p. 391.

that marvellous stories are told of deliverances wrought by her. In the time of Gregory the Great, a fierce pestilence raged in Rome, and thousands of the people perished. The prayers of the Pope failed to procure relief until he ordered a solemn procession in honour of the Virgin, and then the trouble ceased, and " before the end of the procession, an angel was seen on the Tower of Adrian, named ever since, the Castle of St. Angelo, sheathing a bloody sword. At the same moment the angels were heard singing the anthem ' Triumph, oh Queen, Alleluia.' "

"At a monastery of St. Peter, near Cologne, lived a monk perfectly dissolute and irreligious, but very devoted towards the Apostle. Unluckily he died suddenly without confession. The fiends came to seize his soul. St. Peter, vexed at losing so faithful a votary, besought God to admit the monk into Paradise. This prayer was refused, and though the whole body of saints, apostles, angels and martyrs joined at his request to make interest, it was of no avail. In his extremity, he had recourse to the mother of God. ' Fair lady ! ' he said, ' my monk is lost if you do not interfere for him.' The Queen mother assented, and,

followed by all her virgins moved towards her
Son, and the rest may be easily conjectured."
Hallam from whom this story is taken, gives
another, equally well calculated to lead the
sinner to trust in the Virgin as in a Saviour.
A nun ran away from her convent, and for ten
years lived a life of sin. During her absence the
Virgin had filled her place so that her absence
was never noticed. On her return to the convent
she took up her old position, and no one was
aware of her flight. This service was rendered
because, whenever the girl passed an image of
the Virgin, she piously repeated an Ave before it.

We have already indicated what appears to be
the real origin of the worship of the Virgin, and
abundant proof of this can readily be found.
The pictures of the Madonna, by Italian and
Spanish masters, usually represent her as beautifully fair, with blue eyes, and golden hair. But
the prevailing type of beauty in those lands was
very different. The model was Venus, the most
popular of Roman deities, who was usually
painted in this way. If the older sculptures of
Venus and Cupid, and the more modern ones of
the Virgin and Child be compared, little doubt
will remain of the fact, that the later were copies

of the earlier. The common name of the Virgin, Madonna, is simply a translation of a title of the great goddess of Babylon.

The development of the worship of the Virgin is very clearly marked. The first step was the authoritative use of the phrase " Mother of God." Then came the festival of the Assumption ; a feast founded upon a legend that three days after her death her body was carried away to heaven. In the eleventh century such language as this could be used in a sermon preached on the anniversary of that event: " Sovereign Lady of the World! Queen of heaven! Seated at the right hand of God ; all-beautiful, because all-deified ; and placed on the throne of the Trinity." Yet, in some minds, an element of doubt concerning this remained. Was she not, because born of a sinful race, defiled by original sin? And if so, was she a fit object of worship? This was dispelled by the decree of her immaculate conception, by which, it is affirmed, that in her case, sin's entail was miraculously cut off. By a special act of God, she was freed from participation in inherited evil common to the human race. Although the doctrine was not formally and authoritatively announced until 1854, it had for

a long time been accepted as the truth.　Without
any share in inherited sin, and absolutely pure
in conduct, all ground for doubt regarding the
propriety of adoring her is removed.　From the
lavish way in which her praise is sung, and from
the benefits promised those who supplicate her,
it is most difficult to see how any can accept this
teaching and be guiltless of giving to her the
adoration that is due to God only.

CHAPTER X

THE WORSHIP OF IMAGES

WHEN it is remembered that our Saviour lived in a Jewish home, and observed the Jewish law in religious and in social life, it is strange that image worship should be common amongst His followers. If there was one lesson, which, by precept and punishment, God had impressed upon that race, it was that image worship was an abomination. Jesus did not in word condemn the practice because it had ceased for centuries. The temple of Jerusalem was free from visible representations of the Deity; the interior of many Christian churches differ little from heathen shrines.

In pagan communities image worship is common in private and public worship. The Brahmans spend hours daily in their private devotions, before representatives of their gods. It may be a brass image, a shapeless stone, or

10

moulded mud. He treats it as though it were a living and powerful being; going through a series of ceremonies similar to that shown by a host to an honoured guest. He raises it from its couch, bathes it, and then places food before it. If the day is hot, he fans it, if it is cold, he clothes it warmly. With each symbolical act, an appropriate text is recited. In the temples a similar though more elaborate ceremony is observed. On festival days, music and dancing are provided for his amusement. During the hotter part of the day the temple doors are closed to allow the Deity to have rest. What is considered proper for an attendant to do for his master, this in mimic fashion is done for the image. When a man is grateful for favours shown by the god it represents, he is lavish with gifts to the idol; when angry, because his desires remain unfulfilled, he upbraids and punishes it.

If an intelligent man be asked whether the image is really divine, he will reply, that God is in the image as He is in everything else; but that some representation of Him is necessary to secure a definite mental picture. If the ignorant many be questioned, they will unhesitatingly affirm that the image is a living god, and are mortally afraid lest they should kindle its anger.

What is common in Roman Catholic Churches does not greatly differ from this. Beautiful works of art are placed in imposing buildings, as representations of God the Father, the Saviour, the Virgin Mary, and the Saints. Undoubtedly these assist in the formation of clear mental pictures of the beings they represent ; but the All-wise Father, knowing how easily the mind rests on these, rather than on Him who alone is worthy of worship solemnly forbade the making of graven images, and repeatedly punished His people for their disobedience. But, alas, men deem themselves wiser than God. The danger of the practice is fully admitted. A Roman Catholic writer puts the case for their use in this manner. " It is true that the use of these signs (images) becomes dangerous. Formerly God was obliged to forbid it to the Jews, the Christians, however, thought they might without risk imitate their predecessors the Heathen. Serenius, Bishop of Marseilles, in order to preserve the new converts from the guilt of idolatry, destroyed the images in his diocese. But St. Gregory, the Pope, ordered them to be restored, considering that pastoral instruction would correct the grossest of popular errors.[1] Could human presumption go farther? What God forbids, Popes command.

If the practice of placing images for worship in Churches did not come from the teaching of Jesus Christ, nor from Judaism, whence did it arise? There can be but one answer to this question :—it was from the paganism, which Christianity had nominally overcome. In pagan Rome, the temples were adorned with beautiful statues : many of these were destroyed by zealous Christians, others were allowed to remain after receiving Christian names, and in place of those that were destroyed, representations of the Virgin or Saints were substituted.

What is the authoritative teaching of Rome on this question? The creed of Pope Pius IV. says, " I most firmly assert that the images of Christ, of the Ever-Virgin Mother of God, and of other Saints are to be had and retained, and that due honour and veneration are to be rendered to them." In formal phrase it is taught, that there is no honour and reverence due to the

---

[1] Picart, quoted in *Rome Pagan and Papal*, p. 114.

image itself, but only to the being it represents ; but some of Rome's admitted leaders, as we shall see, have taught the very opposite. And even had God not distinctly forbidden it, expediency would have decided against it, when it was known how the heathen regarded their images as divine and living beings.

There is a general consensus of opinion that image worship was unknown in the second century after Christ. It was not until the fifth that it became common. The tombs of the Christians in the Catacombs were adorned with symbols such as the dove, the cross, the good shepherd, etc., but this was a very different matter from the placing of images in the churches. It was chiefly these and similar symbolical ornaments with which the sacred buildings were at first adorned. But in the seventh century this was forbidden, and in their place it was ordered that the Saviour should be represented in human form. From that time the custom has prevailed in the Western Church. But fierce disputes indicate clearly that many saw the evil and stoutly resisted the innovation. In 726, an imperial decree ordered the removal of all images excepting those of the Saviour.

Four years later a far stronger one was issued
declaring the worship of images to be idolatrous,
and threatening with death those who practised
it.   But what the Emperors forbade, Popes
ordered.   The secular power commanded, the
spiritual refused to obey.   The Empress Irene
summoned a Council at Nice in 870, the outcome
of which was that the edicts against image worship were withdrawn.   But her successor being
of a different mind, continued the opposition,
and the Council of Constantinople was called
to settle the matter.   By the decrees of this
assembly whilst pictures were declared to be
permissible, images were forbidden.   The Eastern Church accepted this decision, and to this
day, images are kept out of their churches ;
the Western refused ; and in that section of the
Church, the practice of image worship continues.
As a reason for their removal it was alleged that
their presence hindered the conversion of the
Jews and Mahomedans.

In the Council of Nice, the definition of image
worship was given.   It was stated that " the
worship given to the Virgin and Saints was of
an inferior kind to that which is due to God, and
that the worship was not to be paid to the image,

whether of the Saviour, the Virgin, or the Saint, but to the being, divine or human, whom it represented." But St. Thomas Aqinas affirmed the very opposite. "Since therefore Christ is to be worshipped with the worship of *latria*," (the superior kind of adoration which is due to God) it follows that his image is to be also adored with the worship of *latria*.

In the early centuries, the Christians carefully pointed out to their pagan neighbours the difficulty of restricting their worship to an unseen being, when there was a visible representation of him before them. And yet, after the lapse of years, their descendants ignore this teaching. In a statement made by Cassander to the German Emperor at the time of the Reformation, we have these words, "This worship exhibited to God through images and statues, even the most prudent of the pagans held to be not sufficiently chaste and suitable to God, but invented by superstitious men." And he argues that if pagans felt this, how much more ought Christians to condemn the custom. Athanasius, and other early Christian writers, uttered the sharpest denunciations against what afterward became common in the Church.

Arguing with pagans, they declared that by the use of images they practically denied the omnipresence of their gods, and that a picture of a person, though useful to recall the features of an absent one, was useless when he was present.[1] And further, that a representation of God ought to be living and rational and not a lifeless image, conditions found in the sculptor rather than in the sculpture.

It is alleged that images are " laymen's books," that is, they are for the less cultured members of society. This was practically the defence adopted by the old pagans when attacked by the Christians ; now it is used by Roman Catholic apologists when arguing with Protestants. But, strange to say, although most people are far better educated than their ancestors were, we do not see any diminution in the use of this help for the ignorant. Idolatry has, and ever had, a fatal fascination for the human heart. To condemn the practice that an infallible Church has commanded, would be too flagrant an admission of fallibility. What Rome was, she is, and must continne to be. There appears

---

[1] *Romanism*, p. 220.

to be more hope of ending, than of mending, her.

Certain images are credited with greater efficacy than others, which represent the same being, divine or human. This has led people to believe that some peculiar virtue must inhere in them. This was seen by the more thoughtful of Rome's teachers. In 1787 there was an attempt to check the evil by an assembly of bishops in Tuscany. They drew up a paper in which these words occur, " The honour which is due to images is only founded on the power they possess of representing and recalling the memory of their prototypes. Therefore equal honour is due to all which represent that memory decently, and there cannot, justly, be any distinction between the worship of one image and another."[1] Yet crowds flock to images, concerning which wonderful stories have been put into circulation, imagining that blessings unattainable elsewhere are there to be had for asking. Many shrines of the Virgin are said to possess greater potency than others. The millions of India believe that their great god is

[1] *Romanism*, p. 223.

vastly more gracious at Benares, his favourite
city, than any where else. And legends en-
courage this idea. Interested temple proprietors
have done their best to make them draw ; and
similar means have been used in Christendom.

A hurried description of the specially honoured
images would fill a volume ; all that can be
attempted is to select some of the more conspicuous. It will be seen that in this, as in so
many other matters, the example of the old
paganism has been closely followed.

First of importance is the image of St. Peter
in the magnificent cathedral dedicated to him
in Rome. In an illustrated catologue of the
Vatican, it is said of this statue, "the metal
which previously served for a false divinity,
now serves a sacred and devout use." This
"false divinity" is generally believed to have
been Jupiter, as he was represented on the
Capitoline Hill by a magnificent image. "It is
thus that the Church of Christ converts the
remains of superstition and error to a better
cause ; for whereas before, the metal only
expressed human madness, and the folly of the
Gentiles, the Church now exhibits it as a
monument of faith and devotion. On the

apostle's foot are imprinted the kisses of the people, who assemble there to obtain the indulgences granted by the Roman Pontiff. Remembering that the bronze from which the statue of the Prince of the Apostles was formed, was, in remote times, an ornament of the Capitol, we will add a few words on the object presented to us. Jupiter Capitolinas was so named from the temple of the God on the Capitoline Hall. In one hand he held the thunder, in the other a javelin. He was covered with a purple robe similar to that of the Roman Emperor. In the Vatican Basilica, on various annual solemnities, it is also the custom to clothe the statue of St. Peter in full pontificial dress, and so present it for the worship of the faithful, rich with gold and gems." [1]

Such is the description of this renowned image, wherein in principle, does the later use of the bronze differ from the earlier?

Reference is made to two customs connected with image worship; kissing and clothing the images. Kissing is a very common form of expressing devotion. Sometimes, as in the case

---

[1] *Rome Pagan and Papal*, p. 121.

of St. Peter's image, the lips of the worshipper can touch the toe only ; sometimes the body is kissed from head to foot ; and where the mouth cannot be reached, kisses are thrown by the hand as is common when friends part. As wax images quickly wear away, the part usually kissed, is covered with a metal sheath. In the Church of Sopra Minerva in Rome, a marble statue of the Saviour by Michael Angelo has had to be protected in a similar manner ; though. of late years it has scarcely needed it, as the Virgin's images have almost entirely superseded those of the Christ. In the Augustino and other places, the statues of the Virgin are protected in this way.

Whence has arisen this practice? It is not universal in heathenism. The people are carefully excluded from Hindu temples. Brahmans only being permitted to enter. It was different with Pagan Rome. " In the temple at Agrigentum, " writes Cicero," is a bronze statue of Hercules, than which it would not be easy to find anything more beautiful. Its mouth and chin are slightly worn away, because the people, in their prayers and thanksgiving, are not only in the habit of worshipping, but also of kissing it." Lucretius, who died in the year 55 B.C., tells us that in his day the hands of idols were treated in a similar manner to that which is common now.

> "Then near the door, the reverend statues stand,
>   Worn down and polished is the outstretched hand.
>   So oft the crowd respectful, as they pass
>   Salute and touch the consecrated brass."

The clothing of images on festival days is a common practice. As the Capitoline Jupiter was arrayed in the imperial purple, his successor the Christian Apostle is arrayed in vestments similar to those worn by the Pope. This adorning of statues is not confined to that of St. Peter. It is considered a meritorious act to provide garments and jewels, especially for the images of the Virgin. In the sixth book of Iliad is a graphic account of Hecuba, the Trojan Queen, when seeking help of Pallas, presenting her with the most costly garments obtainable. In heathen Rome the people regarded the images as living, and made offerings of a kind such as they imagined would be welcome to them. In Christian Rome a similar superstition leads to a similar practice.

There are other ceremonies that seem equally
strange until the customs prevailing in Christendom anterior to the establishment of Christianity
are known, then the mystery disappears. On
days devoted to the worship of a saint, an image,
or it may be a relic representing it, is carried
through the streets. Priests, soldiers, bands of
music, banners, etc., are called into use ; in fact,
whatever is calculated to gather and impress a
crowd. The image is taken to pay a visit of
respect to another church, and on its return, a
bountiful feast is spread before it. In times of
calamity, as special help is wanted, special processions are got up to secure it. In a precisely
similar manner on days devoted to the deities,
the images of the old gods of Rome were treated.
What is pleasing to themselves they imagined
would please the deity; hence the universal
feasting on such occasions. As the temples were
usually closed for a few hours in the afternoon,
whilst the gods were having their siesta, the
churches are closed to-day. If the gods were
unpropitious, their images were cursed, beaten,
reproached. On the death of Germanicus, the
people were so angry that they pelted the images
with stones ; and Augustus took revenge on

Neptune for the loss of his fleet by refusing to allow his image to be carried in the procession to the games which followed shortly afterwards. To-day it is common for the images to be ill-treated when the saints represented by them have not been gracious to the suppliants.

There are images in various parts of Christendom said to work miracles in the sight of their adorers. It is a significant fact that there is scarcely one which has not its original in old Rome. Has an image of the Virgin been seen to weep? To this power of the gods of his day Lucan alludes, when speaking of the prodigies that occurred during the civil wars :—

> " Tears shed by gods, our country's patrons,
>   And sweat from Lares, told the city's woes."

Virgil too refers to similar wonders :—

> " The weeping statues did the wars foretell
>   And holy sweat from brazen idols fell."

When in the consulship of Appius Claudius Publius Crassus was slain in battle, Apollo's statue at Cumœ shed tears for four days without intermission. If a Madonna can wink, the images of paganism can laugh. Has an image of the Virgin the power to look benignantly on her worshippers and send them home happy? The image of the Egyptian Isis was so constructed that the silver snake on her forehead could shake." [1]

In a previous chapter mention has been made of the miraculous manner in which some images have been transferred from one place to another. Probably the story of an image of Cybele was the original. The vessel which brought it to Rome ran aground at the mouth of the Tiber. Nothing could move her, until a girl, whose purity had been questioned, tied her veil to it. Being able to tow it into the city by so slender a rope, her innocence was proved beyond question.

As a rule, the images of the Virgin represent her as beautiful and attractive in appearance. At Auvergne there is a black image of the Madonna as ugly as an artist could make it. Probably in former days there was a popular local deity represented in this form, whose worship was superseded by this unique image of the "Queen of Heaven." In a similar manner

[1] *The Two Baylons*, 377.

in India, the goddess Durgā, beautiful in form, and attractive in appearance, as she is represented at one season of the year, at another her image is black, and her appearance as savage and cruel, as can be imagined. It is known that this repulsive image is a representation of a goddess once commonly worshipped in Bengal, upon the cult of which that of the more benignant looking Durgā was grafted. Now they are declared to be differing forms of the same deity. Might not a Roman Catholic prelate have said of the whole system what he was bold enough to say of the Cathedral of Orvieto, where classic deities and Christian saints are represented side by side," this is paganised Christianity ? "

CHAPTER XI

THE VENERATION OF RELICS

IN the Creed of Pius IV. it is declared "that the relics of the Saints are to be venerated." When Dr. Manning was about to establish a branch of the Order of St. Charles in England, he visited Milan, the head-quarters, to learn all he could about the saint, and the rules of the institution. In a letter to Cardinal Wiseman, he said "the Archibishop received me very kindly, and has given me two relics of the blood of St. Charles. There was no portion of the body to be obtained." About forty years ago, the Pope, as a special favour, gave what was declared to be a tooth of St. Peter, to the Emperor of Austria.

Very early in the Christian era the tombs of the martyrs were regarded as specially sacred. To them the persecuted resorted for prayer, that by the remembrance of their faithfulness, they might be kept stedfast. By a short step,

not the place of interment only, but part of the
saint's body, or property, came to be regarded
as worthy of veneration. Over their tombs
churches were erected ; and in more distant
places, others were built to commemorate
them and under the altar their relics were
treasured. So desireable did the Church consider this practice, that by the Second Council
of Nice, in the year 787, a decree was made
forbidding the consecration of a Church unless
relics could be obtained. The greater the
number of such treasures, and the greater the
saint to whom they had belonged, the more
holy the building in which they were enshrined·
Wonderful stories of miracles wrought by these
remains were circulated, and many came to
secure the benefit obtainable from them. Lecky
has called attention to the fact, that, as knowledge spreads, the accounts of miracles become
less frequent, until they entirely cease, and
quotes an ingenious explanation of this from
Bishop Spratt. " God never left Himself without a witness in the world ; and, it is observable,
that he has usually chosen the dark and ignorant
ages, wherein to work miracles, but seldom or
never times when natural knowledge prevailed

For He knew that there was not so much need
of extraordinary signs, when men were diligent
in the works of His hands, and attentive to the
impression of his footsteps in His creatures."[1]

It is not easy to say exactly when the transition
from simple reverence for the faithful witnesses
was made to an idolatrous veneration of their
remains. The belief in the resurrection of the
body led the early Christians to bury rather that
burn their dead.   And the martyrs especially,
they were anxious to honour with decent burial.
Probably it was during the age of persecution
that the evil spread rapidly ; so that in a short
time, what was to the more intelligent a mere
memento of an honoured disciple of Jesus Christ,
was treated by the more ignorant with the same
respect, and accredited with even greater power
than its owner had exercised during life.   In
the Acts of Fructuosi, who died in the year 259,
the friends of the martyrs are forbidden to retain
any relics. When a martyrdom took place the
Christians came by night to carry off the charred
remains. But, it is said, the saint appeared to
forbid this practice. Though the earliest mention

Rise and Influence of Rationalism in Europe, I. p. 145.

of the veneration of relics is in the fourth century, it is probable that it originated at an earlier date. From that time stories of miracles wrought by relics increase in number and extravagance.

That the people should venerate, and even worship such things, can scarcely be wondered at, when we read the words of their religious teachers. Chrysostom says "Let us fall down before their remains, let us embrace their coffins, for the coffins of the martyr's acquire great virtue. The bones of the martyrs drive away disease, and put death to flight. Where the bones of the martyrs are, the devils fly as from fire." St. Basil declared "that from the tomb of Juletta at Cæsarea, a spring of water issued, which was a safeguard in health, and a comfort to the sick." At Arles, in order that the whole city should benefit by the remains of Genesius, his blood was allowed to remain where it fell, but his body was carried to the district on the opposite side of the river. St. Augustine solemnly affirms that "in his own diocese at Hippo, in two years only, no less than seventy miracles had been wrought by the body of St. Stephen ; and that in the neighbouring Province of Calama, where the relic had previously been preserved, the number was incomparably greater. He gives a catalogue of what he deems undoubted miracles, selected from a multitude so great, that volumes would be required to relate them. In that catalogue we find no less than five cases of restoration of life to the dead."[1] When Bishop Projectius brought the relics of St. Stephen to Aquæ Tibulitinæ, the people came in crowds to welcome them. Amongst these was a blind woman, to whom the Bishop gave some flowers which she pressed to her eyes and was able to see. Another story, as told by Augustine, is as follows; A tailor who had lost his coat, and was too poor to buy another, went to the shrine of the twenty martyrs, and asked their help. As he left the place, a number of boys made fun of him, asking what the martyrs had done for him. Walking along he saw a fish lying panting on the shore. This he sold to a cook, and went home, hoping to get a new garment. But soon afterwards, the man who had bought the fish, came to the tailor with a gold ring which he had found inside it. Thus the man's

[1] *Rise and Influence of Rationalism*, I. p. 163.

prayer was answered more generously than even he had expected. [1]

Such stories are not confined to a far distant past. "In 1870, an Italian lady afflicted with incipient cancer, was exhorted by a Jesuit priest to commend herself to the Blessed John Berchmans, a pious Jesuit novice of Belguim, who died in 1621, and was beatified in 1865. Her adviser procured for her three small packets of dust from the coffin of this saintly innocent, a little cross was made from the boards of the coffin the blessed youth occupied, as well as some portion of the wadding in which his venerable head was wrapped. During nine days' devotion, the patient accordingly invoked the Blessed John, swallowed small portions of his dust in water, and at last pressed the cross to her breast so vehemently that she was seized with sickness, went to sleep, and awoke without a symptom of the complaint." [2]

The bones of the Old Testament saints were regarded as unclean by the Jews and converts from Judaism; but in the fourth century the attitude

[1] *The Two Babylons*, p. 258

[2] Taylor's *Primitive Culture*, ii. p. 112.

of Christians towards them was very different.
In a letter to Marcella, written by Paula in the
year 386, it is suggested that on her visit to the
Holy Land, she should pray at David's tomb,
hasten to the tabernacles of Abraham, Isaac, and
Jacob; visit Samaria and adore the ashes of
John the Baptist, Elisha, and Obadiah. Jerome
affirms that Arcadius translated the bones of the
prophet Samuel from Judæa to Thrace. By the
aid of Charlemagne the following relics are said
to have been found: the blood, hair, and
garments of John the Baptist, the bones of
Zacharias, some memorials of Simeon. In the
fourteenth century it is affirmed that some of
Noah's beard was on view.

Of our Saviour, as might have been expected,
there are many relics reverenced. The wood of
His cross was naturally an object to be desired;
and it is affirmed, on good authority, that of this,
enough could be collected from churches in
Christendom to make many. The teachers of
the Church do not deny it, but explain how it
has come about. It has been miraculously
increased by God, as the bread increased in the
hands of the disciples in order that the multitudes
might have food in the desert. The reed on

which a sponge was offered Him, as He hung upon the cross, as also the sponge itself; the nails which pierced his hands and feet; the pillar against which He leaned whilst He was scourged; the thorns of His crown are all somewhere to be seen; whilst his garments have multiplied indefinitely; no less than twenty cathedrals have professed to be in possession of His seamless robe. A reliquary at Corbie is especially rich in relics of our Lord, as it is affirmed that it contains some of His blood and hair; the manger in which He lay, the napkin that was about His head in the tomb, part of His cross, and some of His garments.

As the body of the Virgin was said to be carried to heaven three days after her death there are but few relics of her to be had. Amongst others, it may be mentioned, that what professes to be her hair, her milk, her girdle, her veil, and shreds of her garments, are carefully preserved in various places. The most important relic of her is her home, which was miraculously conveyed from Syria to Italy.

The heads of St. Peter and St. Paul, and portions of their bodies, are said to be kept at the Churches sacred to them in Rome. But the most wonderful relic is a cloth, with which a few drops of water were wiped up, which fell from the robes of St. Stephen when he appeared in a vision to a man on board a ship in distress.

As the demand for relics increased, the supply proportionately increased. Many made profit from the sale, and others made profit from their exhibition. In some instances, articles professedly worthy of veneration were rejected, because they could not stand the tests that were applied.

Our own country furnishes a typical story of relic finding. Tradition teaches that St. Alban was the first Christian martyr in Britain. He was a Roman citizen who was put to death in the Diocletian persecution for harbouring a friend. On the spot where he was put to death, the cathedral now stands. There is no real proof that St. Alban or his friend ever lived; the name of the friend being Amphibolus, and may mean his cloak.

In the year 793 the Church and monastery were founded by the Saxon King Offa, as an atonement for the guilt of murder. Relics were wanted for the consecration. Some one dreamed that St. Alban's bones were to be found in a certain place. Priests and people marched in solemn procession to the spot, and a light flash from heaven indicated exactly where the excavation should be made.   A box was found, and the sacred remains transferred to the Cathedral.   In the shrine are holes, where the limbs or clothes of the sick were able to reach the saint's remains, by whose virtue they hoped to regain health.

Some years later, doubts arose amongst the monks regarding these relics. As one of these doubters was reciting the evening service in honour of the saint, he was terrified at seeing a stranger who said, " I am Albanus !   Didst thou not see me come from the tomb ? "   This settled the matter.   Further proof was unnecessary.

It was not until the sixteenth century that there was any serious condemnation of relic hunting and relic worship.   Attempts had been made to regulate it.   In 675 a Council condemned the custom of Bishops marching in procession before relics as though they were the ark of the Lord ; but at the Council of Trent it was encouraged rather than condemned.

A meeting for prayer and praise at the scene of an act of heroism, or the erection of a church, to commemorate an act of fidelity to conscience is innocent and beneficial. But when a church cannot be consecrated without relics; or when they are held up for veneration, and people flock to them for healing, they cease to be innocent aids to devotion. To many they are idols, and their veneration idolatry. Most strange it is that men can believe a lifeless bone to have greater power for good than a living man. It is another form of the superstition that the dead are more powerful than the living. The Romish Church, rather than correct this, has made use of it as a means of filling her coffers.

Was the veneration of relics original? It was not apostolic, nor Jewish, but it was pagan. Plutarch tells the story of Cimon searching for the bones of Theseus. Seeing an eagle tearing up the earth, he took this for a heavenly sign where to dig, and was rewarded by the sight of the hero's body. Athens rejoiced at the discovery, erected a splendid building to receive them, and set apart a day to commemorate their recovery. The shoulder bone of Pelops was indicated by an oracle as a means of saving the Eleans from a pestilence. The Thebans preserved the bones of Hector, as a means of securing prosperity. In Egypt, such was the demand for relics of their gods, that many cities had arms and legs of the same Deity.

In Hinduism reverence for relics is not common. The custom of burning the dead has largely deprived the people of these treasures. Moreover, according to their system, contact with a dead body is defiling. But there are two notable exceptions to this rule.

The goddess Parvati committed suicide, and her husband, mad with grief, wandered about with her dead body. As this caused great trouble, a god named Vishnu cut it into fifty pieces, and wherever a part fell, a temple grew to honour it. These buildings are hundreds of miles apart; but it is the relic contained in them that gives them peculiar sanctity. As Puri, in the celebrated temple of Jagannātha, it is affirmed that the bones of Krishna, a Hindu deity, are enshrined. This place was the chief centre of Buddhism; but when the older Hinduism re-asserted itself, and the Buddhists were persecuted, the shrine of the heterodox worship was made attractive to the orthodox, by placing within the image the relics of the Hindu god.

But in Buddhism, the veneration of relics, to

say the least, is as prominent as in the Roman Catholic Church. As a rule, these are preserved in buildings erected specially for their preservation, rather than in temples. In a standard work is an account of the erection of a Dagoba, as these reliquaries are called. As soon as it was ready, the master of the ceremonies is said to have sprung into the air, to the height of seven palm trees, and brought down a casket containing the dress of Buddha, which he laid aside on entering the priesthood. This was solemnly placed in its shrine. In various places, Buddha's teeth, nails, bones, hair, are sacredly preserved, and on festival days exhibited. Many miracles are said to have been wrought by them. Some time after his death, an attempt was made to collect his scattered limbs, and an annual festival is held to commemorate that event. In its main features, the veneration of relics is very similar in Christendom and heathendom.

CHAPTER XII

SHRINES AND PILGRIMS

THE idea that special sanctity attaches to certain places, where blessings unattainable elsewhere may be secured, is common in paganism. Nor is this surprising. Believing in many gods, by an offering at one shrine the aid of one deity is invoked; at another shrine quite a different being. These may be not merely unfriendly but positively hostile to each other. But it is surprising that those who believe in an Almighty Father should adopt similar methods; and especially when this practice was distinctly condemned by the Saviour. In answer to the woman of Samaria, who affirmed that her people considered that district most suitable for worship, whilst the Jew considered Jerusalem peculiarly holy, He said, "The hour cometh when ye shall neither in this mountain, nor yet in Jerusalem, worship the Father."

In India, as in other non-Christian lands, shrines are numerous. Some enjoy only a local fame; others attract people from most distant parts of the country. Different boons are sought at different places; by visiting many, almost every good for this life and the next, can, it is hoped, be obtained. And there are Christian shrines almost perfectly analagous. In both cases touts are employed, or other means used to advertise them. Shrine management is a lucrative business. The more visitors, the greater the income.

The Ganges is regarded as a holy and sanctifying river throughout its entire length; but four places are superlatively so. To these pilgrims go in myriads. The source of the stream, where the melted snow from the lofty peaks of the Himalayahs, rushes into the plains; Allahabad, where two branches unite; Benares where the great god has his favourite earthly home; and Saugor Island, where river and sea meet. It is the boon of salvation that the visitors hope to secure by bathing. Rightly understood, it is not deliverance from the love and power of sin that is sought, but deliverance from the penalty of sin. Bathing is an act of merit, which can be employed as a set-off against offences. Of the river shrines Benares is by far the most important. Fully two-thirds of the people met there are pilgrims. Some go for a few days only, others remain for years, and others are carried there to die. The great god, in a fit of anger, cut off one of the Creator's heads. This stuck to his hand until he came in sight of the city. Delighted that he had, at last, lost the sign of his sin, he promised salvation to all who visited, and a speedy entrance into heaven to those who died there.

There is another place, Puri, where salvation is promised to the visitor. There the boon is to be obtained by seeing the image of the god. The greater gods united their energies to endow this shrine in order that there might be a means whereby the greatest sinner could obtain deliverance, no matter against whom the offence was committed.

Other shrines promise deliverance from bodily sickness. To these the blind and dumb, the lame and halt, the leper and epileptic go in crowds to bathe in a filthy pond, and drink polluted water. Stories of their healing virtue are circulated by interested people ; but it is difficult to find any who have derived benefit. The suffering ones

12

present admit that their troubles remain, but are comforted with the assurance that the virtue of the visit will be experienced on their return home. Many of these shrines have been celebrated for centuries; but occasionally new ones are added

There is another class of religious resorts that should be mentioned; those to which pilgrims go to benefit their ancestors rather than themselves. Gāya, in North India, is visited annually by large numbers of people who go there to perform part of the ceremonies for the dead, under the impression that they will then exert far greater influence than if performed at home. Not only the person who has recently died, but remoter ancestors are said to be greatly benefitted in this way.

There are Christian Shrines where almost identical benefits are expected. First come those visited with the hope of getting salvation from sin. In christian countries, as in heathen, it is deliverance from the penalty rather than the power of sin that is promised. Indulgences are the reward of all who make a pilgrimage to them : and an indulgence is simply the remission of the punishment attached to sin. In the lette authorizing Tetzel to sell them to enrich the revenues of Rome, we learn what benefit they promise. "We, Leo, have granted John Tetzel the most ample power of communicating indulgences, so that he can absolve in all cases, specially and generally, and in any manner so ever, reserved to the Roman Apostolic See, such as the same See would be rightly consulted upon. Also of absolving from sins repented of, confessed, and forgotten, and even from those not repented of, and not confessed ; and, in the moment of death, of bestowing a universal remission of all sins, guilt, and penalty to be paid in Purgatory. Also to shut the gates of hell, and to open the gate of Paradise."[1] Can human presumption surpass this? God promises pardon to the penitent ; the Pope offers it, for a money consideration, to the impenitent. The Hindu promise is that the act of bathing will remove all sin, past, present, and future. The Pope's indulgences promise practically the same blessing. At any rate sins as yet uncommitted can be cancelled by them.

The Pope grants indulgences to those who

[1] *Romanism*, p. 235.

visit certain churches, repeat a prayer before an image, or crowd to see a reputed relic of our Saviour or a saint. Superstitious people fulfil the condition under the impression that they can escape from the penalty attached to sin. They trust in God for deliverance from the condemnation of hell, they buy, by money or service, an indulgence to free them from the lesser punishment. When a Japanese pilgrim visits a temple at the foot of the sacred mountain, he receives a stamped certificate, which, in his estimation, is a passport to heaven, as a similar document with an official stamp, is a passport to the town he wishes to visit. In principle it is difficult to see wherein the Christian method of salvation is superior to the Buddhist. The origin of the Roman Catholic system of obtaining money by the sale of pardons, very probably was a practice of the Emperor Vespasian. When he was in need of funds, he filled his coffers by selling pardons to criminals.

As an illustration of the shrines to which pilgrims are attracted by the promise of an indulgence, the Cathedral of Treves may be mentioned. The authorities there have what is called "The Holy Coat," the seamless robe

of our Saviour which he wore up to the time of
the crucifixion, and for which the soldiers cast
lots. The Empress Helena, mother of Constantine, is said to have acquired it during a
visit to Jerusalem, and to have given it to the
Cathedral where it is now kept. By many it is
implicitly believed that this garment is what it
professes to be, and is worshipped accordingly.
Strange to say the first wrttten notice of this
treasure is eight centuries after the time when
it was discovered. The lady who found it is also
credited with finding the Cross of Calvary. She
went to secure relics, and she secured them, or
what served her purpose as well. Legends of
an extravagant character have been multiplied
about this robe. The Virgin Mary, it is said,
spun the cloth. Herod gave it to a Jew, who
cast it into the sea. A holy pilgrim recovered
it, but because he was nnworthy to possess
such a sacred treasure, he threw it back into the
sea, and it was swallowed by a whale. In due
time the whale was caught, and the garment
was purchased by the King of Treves, for the
thirty pieces of silver paid to Judas for betraying
his Master, this money being supplied by the
Virgin Mary. Once in about fifty years it is

exposed to view, and about two millions of
people file before it. In special cases the sick
are allowed to touch the glass case in which it is
kept; but this favour is not easily obtained. An
indulgence of seven years is promised to those
who see it, which indulgence can be enjoyed
by the pilgrims themselves or transferred to a
soul in Purgatory.

As an illustration of Christian superstition
similar to that which leads a Hindu to visit a
shrine rather than a physician in case of sickness,
the pilgrimage to Lourdes may be given. In
1858 a girl declared that she saw a vision of the
Virgin Mary, which was repeated several times.
At last the Virgin informed her that a spring of
water running near by had miraculous powers of
healing, and sent a message to the priest of the
village to build a church. Eventually this was
done, and the fame of the place has rapidly
grown, until now there is an annual pilgrimage
mostly of sick folk and their friends. The
methods employed are similar to those in
India :—the drinking of the water, and bathing
the affected parts with it. Careful examination,
by trustworthy and disinterested parties, proves
that a few of those who go are benefitted; but

the sufferings of most are increased by the long journey, and discomforts of the place. Stories of faith healing, where no outward and visible means for recovery are employed, are as wonderful as the reported cures at Lourdes. The excitement of travel, the general commotion at the shrine, the stories of miraculous cures which are recited, and the expectation of good, will account for most, at any rate, of the restorations with which "Our Lady of Lourdes" is credited.

As an instance in the Romish Church, where a shrine is resorted to rather for the benefit of the dead than the living, may be given that at New Pompeii, an interesting account of which is found in the "Sunday at Home" for 1894. As Don Bartolo the founder of the Church of the Madonna of the Rosary was standing in his field at vesper-time, the Virgin and child appeared to him in a vision, and then he saw a Church, around which a city grew. From that moment he set to work to make the vision a reality. First came the building of the church, and then the providing a suitable picture to adorn it, before which the faithful might bow. The story of the discovery and purchase of this picture, the most sacred and adorable object in the church, has features in it, ludicrous in the extreme, if they were not almost blasphemous. It was found in an old curiosity shop, touched up by an artist, the original saints around the central figure being painted out, while others were painted in to take their place. It was at first set up in an unfinished form, but as funds came, improvements were made.

In connection with this Church, and as an inducement to people to flock there, several forms of indulgence are offered. One is to this effect, "in the Sanctuary of Pompeii whosoever hears a mass at the altar of St. Joseph obtains plenary indulgence, and the liberation of a soul from Purgatory." Another, "On the day of the apparition of St. Michael there is plenary indulgence for those who visit the Church, or hear a mass, together with the liberation of souls from Purgatory."

Whence has come the idea that blessings are more easily obtained at certain places? Surely not from Him who taught "if ye being evil know how to give good gifts unto your children, how much more shall your Father which is in heaven give good things to them that ask

Him." It is simply the result of old superstitions; of the old heathen idea that God is not spontaneously gracious, but may be made so by gifts and suffering. The following account of St. Teodoro's Church in Rome furnishes an illustration of the way in which a heathen shrine has been changed into a Christian one, retaining the old inducements to pilgrims to visit it. " It is curious to note in Rome how many a modern superstition has its root in an ancient one, and how tenaciously custom still clings to the old localities. On the Capitoline Hill, the bronze she-wolf was once worshipped as the wooden bambino is now. It stood in the temple of Romulus, and thither the ancient Romans used to carry children to be cured of their diseases by touching it. On the supposed site of the temple now stands the church dedicated to St. Teodoro. Though names have changed, and the temple has vanished, and church after church have decayed and been rebuilt, the old superstition remains, and the common people, at certain periods, still bring their sick children to the Saint that he may heal them with his touch."[1]

[1] Hare's *Walks in Rome*, i. p. 233.

In old Rome the people went to the temples
of the deity, who was supposed to be able to
assist in the way help was wanted. For a good
harvest Ceres was propiated ; for the deliverance
of their friends from hell, Pluto's aid was asked ;
those about to brave the sea, committed themselves to the care of Neptune. As there would
not be within reach of all a temple of every god
whose blessing they desired, pilgrimages became
necessary. To meet this old superstitious desire
in the hearts of those who had not learned that
the Father was ever near, special shrines were
provided, and worshippers attracted by the
promise of benefits.

CHAPTER XIII

RELIGIOUS FESTIVALS

IN non-Christian communities, the sacredness of the Sabbath is unknown, but on days devoted to the worship of certain deities the people wholly or partially abstain from their ordinary work that they may visit the temples, or be present at worship in their homes. A similar practice was common in ancient Rome, for the poets charged the people with neglecting the duties of the house, the farm, the mart, in order that they might assist at these festivals of the gods.

In considering the Christian Festivals which have supplanted the pagan, first in order will be those connected with our Lord, then those of the Virgin, and finally those of the Saints.

1. Festivals connected with the life of our Lord.

Christmas Day.

Probably most Christians imagine that Jesus Christ was born on December 25th. It has been their practice from infancy to associate that great event with that day. As a matter of fact, the year, much less the month of the nativity is not known. This, however, with confidence may be affirmed, that it was not in the year I of the Christian era, nor was it on December 25th of any year. During the first century no special festival marked the day, the first certain trace of it is about the middle of the second century. A few years later it was observed in many parts of the Empire; in some places, January, in others, the Spring, and in yet others, December was the time selected. The main argument against December, being the month of the Saviour's birth is based on the fact, that, at that season shepherds do not watch their flocks by night on the plains, as the weather is too cold and wet for them to be exposed. Dr. Kitto says, "It is clear that a celebration of the day of Christ's nativity was not thought of in the earliest days of the Christian Church. When it was at last considered proper,

no clue or tradition existed as to the real time,
which had to be determined by probabilities, of
which we are as competent judges as the
founders of the festival were; and perhaps more
competent, from the more severely critical
tendencies of our age.   We strongly think that
there is no satisfactory evidence of the time of
year, and still less as to the precise day; and, it
appears to us, that the season, and consequently
the day, have been determined on erroneous and
uncritical data."   Clement of Alexandria, in the
middle of the third century, expressed the
opinion that the attempt to fix the year and day
was "futile and impracticable."   In the Eastern
Church no mention of it is found before the fourth
century; and it was decided to join the celebration of the Saviour's birth with that of the
Epiphany on January 6th, on which date it is
still observed.   Sir Isaac Newton suggested that
the great festivals of the church were designedly
distributed to the cardinal points of the year;
the Annunciation Day being in the Spring, St.
John's birth in the Summer, St. Michael's in the
Autumn, and Christ's birth at Christmas.   The
general opinion seems to be that the Nativity
was in September, about the time of the Feast

of Tabernacles.   The harvest then being
gathered in, the people were free to go up to the
centres to which they belonged for the census
ordered by the Emperor.

A study of the ceremonies common at
Christmas will indicate that it is a perpetuation
of a popular heathen festival.   Centuries before
our Lord's birth, Dec. 25, was regarded as a
specially holy day.   On it was celebrated the
birth of a deity in Babylon, and Egypt, and in
Greece and Rome who derived their religious
knowledge from them.   It was the time when
the sun started on a new circle; this, in poetic
language, was called his birth.   The visible sun
was the representative of the invisible god who
made it.   The feast fixed for this day, celebrated
the birth of God on earth.   It continued for
several days, and was a time of drunkenness and
revelry.   Slaves were free during its continuance,
and ruled their masters, as in the dark ages
of Europe there was a "lord of misrule," who
presided over the amusements at Christmas.
The burning of candles, the Christmas tree, the
Yule log, the boar's head, as part of the feast,
were all found in the older festival ; and all had
symbolic meaning.   In the decking of our homes

with evergreens there is the continuance of a custom which prevailed in far off days ; by this means our fathers expressed their faith in the power of the sun to renew the face of nature.

What has here been said must not be regarded as a condemnation of a proper observance of the Christmas feast ; but as an illustration of the wholesale borrowing of pagan ceremonies by the Church. We do well to give thanks to the Father that He gave his Son to save the world ; to rejoice that the Infinitely Great condescended to appear on earth as a child. But the Christmas ceremonies in a Roman Catholic Church, if not idolatrous, it is difficult to see wherein they differ from idolatry. In a brilliantly lighted building, with attractive music, the sacred drama of the Saviour's birth is enacted. The stable, the manger, and the infant are on view. As the wooden image is raised aloft, the choir sing, " Glory to God in the Highest," and the people bow in solemn adoration. Of course the more intelligent know that the image is merely representative ; the young and ignorant regard it as divine. When Aaron made the calf in the wilderness, the people knew it was made of the gold they had given ; but their action was an offence to the Almighty, and brought upon them severe punishment. A stranger watching Christians in Church, and heathen before a shrine would be unable to see any difference in their attitude towards their visible representations of the Divine.

Easter Day

In other Christian lands this is known as the Passover Feast; it being held at the time the Jews observe their great festival to commemorate the deliverance God wrought for their forefathers. How is it that it bears another name in this country? The early Missionaries found that our ancestors had a great feast at this season. They rejoiced in the victory Spring had gained over Winter, and that the time had come for the budding of the leaf, the singing of the birds, the manifestation of renewed life. This feast bore the name of Easter, and was connected with the worship of Baal and Astarte, as some ceremonies still observed clearly indicate. On their conversion to Christianity, the older festival with its familiar name was retained. The God of heaven was substituted for Baal, and the people were taught to celebrate the Resurrection of our Lord in addition to the return of the spring. That the worship of Baal was at one time prevalent in this country the following account of what takes place annually near Crieff will show : " A number of men and women, assemble at an ancient Druidical circle of stones at Baltaire. They light a fire, and each person puts a bit of oatcake in a shepherd's bonnet. The people, blindfolded, draw a piece of the cake from the bonnet, one of which has been blackened. Whoever draws this has to jump through the fire and pay a forfeit. This is part of the ancient worship of Baal, and the person thus chosen by lot was previously burned as a sacrifice. Passing through the fire represents that ; and the payment of the forfeit redeems the victim." [1]

Corpus Christi Festival

This was ordained to call attention to the stupendous miracle of transforming the wafer and wine into the Body and Blood of our Lord.   It

[1] *The Two Babylons*, p. 148.

13

was founded in the year 1264 by Pope Urban
IV., and is celebrated on the Thursday after
Trinity Sunday. The Host is carried through
the streets in solemn procession, and an opportunity given to those, who do not attend Mass,
to adore it. Indulgences are liberally promised
to all who properly keep this feast:—Two
hundred days to those who attend matins; forty
to those who are present at the later services;
and two hundred to those who take part in the
preparatory services on the eight days preceding.

The origin of it is as follows. Whilst Urban
was staying at Orvieto, the report of a wonderful
miracle at Bolsena reached him. It should be
noted that although the doctrine of Transubstantiation had been taught for fifty years, it
was not universally accepted. A young priest,
who was somewhat sceptical about this great
dogma, whilst celebrating mass at Bolsena, saw
blood flowing from the broken wafer, and
bubbling from the cup. Of course he was converted, and went to tell the Pope. By the Pope's
order, the Bishop of Orvieto fetched the wafer,
and the linen on which the blood fell. These
were solemnly exhibited, and who could then
doubt? The splendid cathedral of Orvieto was

built in commemoration of the event.[1] In 1264 a Bull was issued ordering the perpetual observance of the Festival of Corpus Christi. In the Cathedral are frescoes vividly representing the miracle which quickened faith in the great doctrine. The Church contains figures of heathen deities side by side with Christian saints, and a Roman Catholic official admitted to a sturdy Protestant that it was a structure of "paganized Christianity."

The Invention or Discovery and the Elevation or Exaltation of the Cross. The former is held on May 3rd, the latter on Sept. 14th. In the year 326, Helena, the mother of the Emperor Constantine, undertook a pilgrimage to Palestine, to visit the places sacred through their association with the Saviour. She was nearly eighty years of age when she set out. She first tried to find the sepulchre. This was covered to a considerable depth with rubbish. On the removal of this, three crosses were found, and, what was declared to be, the inscription Pilate placed on that of the Saviour. The question as to which of the crosses was the one

[1] *Rome Pagan and Papal*, p. 224.

on which the Saviour died was settled by miracle. A sick person touched all three ; but recovery was effected by one only. At the same time the nails which had pierced His hands and feet were also found. One half of the cross was left in Jerusalem in a Church built specially to enshrine it ; the other half was divided between Constantinople and Rome. In following years pieces of the cross were given to specially holy pilgrims ; but there was no perceptible diminution of the original wood. When the Persians conquered Jerusalem, they carried off the cross. Fourteen years later they restored it ; the second festival is to commemorate its return to its shrine. The circumstances attendant on the discovery of the cross throw discredit upon the story. It was an uncritical age. Miracles are reported to induce faith in the result of the search. It is a notorious fact that in the present enlightened age archæologists, notwithstanding the care with which they examine desired relics, are frequently imposed upon.

II. Festivals of the Virgin.

As the worship of the Virgin is so universal

and popular, it is natural that her festivals should be numerous and attractive. There are four that call for notice.

The Nativity of the Virgin.

This though first in order, is not the first in importance. Its origin dates back only to the year 1683. When Vienna was besieged by the Moors, a fire broke out near an arsenal. Had this exploded, a breach in the walls would have been made. The help of the Virgin was sought, and, as the threatened evil was averted, it was attributed to her intercession. This happened on the eve of the Festival of the Assumption, and was regarded as the birthday of the Virgin, and a new festival was inaugurated to commemorate it.

The Annunciation.

This, the great festival of the Virgin, is celebrated on Lady Day, and is intended to commemorate the visit of the angel, informing her that she was to be the mother of our Lord. In the early days of the Church, no attempt was made to mark this day as specially important ; but when it was decreed that the birth of Jesus should be celebrated on Dec. 25th, the 25th of March was taken as the date of the angel's visit, and duly honoured. On this day, a feast had been kept many centuries before in honour of Cybele, the mother of the Babylonish Messiah. This was now restored ; even the titles of the heathen goddess being transferred to Mary. She was known in Rome's pagan days as Domina, the lady ; from this the common term Madonna has come.

The Assumption.

According to the teaching of the Romish Church, the body of the Virgin was "assumed," or taken to heaven, three days after her death : this festival was appointed to celebrate the event. Her resurrection was ante-dated. But grave doubts concerning this were entertained by many. They asked, how can an evil body enter into the presence of a holy God. Mary's body, by natural descent from Adam, was tainted with original sin. To remove this uncertainty, in 1854, it was authoritatively taught, that she was freed from inherited evil by a divine act The decree is as follows: "We declare, pronounce, and define, that the doctrine which holds that the Blessed Virgin Mary, at the first instant of her conception, by the singular privilege and grace of the omnipotent God, in virtue of the merits of Jesus Christ, the Saviour of the world, was preserved immaculate from all stains of original sin, has been revealed by God, and therefore should be firmly, and constantly believed by the faithful." Such is the teaching of the infallible Church to-day, although the doctrine has been vehemently opposed by some of the holiest and most learned of her teachers. Some have gone so far as to charge with mortal sin those who attend services in which the doctrine is taught and commemorated. In addition to the reason given above, it is held that this dogma is needed to support the belief in the sinlessness of Jesus. If His mother, from whom He obtained His human body, was not free from sin, how could he be absolutely pure?

The idea of the deification of the human was familiar to the early converts. The Emperors after death, and in some cases during their life, were regarded as divine. It was not an original conception that man could be made into a god, nor that a body could be assumed, and permitted to enter heaven. Bacchus is said to have rescued her mother from the powers of darkness, and carried her in triumph to heaven. Of Porsepine, daughter of Ceres, it was common to speak, as "the holy Virgin," and of her it was affirmed, that she was "not only free from actual sin, but pure in essence, and immaculately conceived."[1] In the titles given to the Virgin, in her festivals, and in the attendant ceremonies, there is a striking resemblance to what was common in heathen Rome.

The Purification.

This is to commemorate the visit of the holy mother to the temple after the birth of her son. At first it is not easy to see why any great prominence should have been given to this act. There can, however, be little doubt that the feast was arranged to take the place of an older festival in honour of Ceres. In pagan days, processions

[1] *The Two Babylons*, p. 183.

marched through the fields, and offerings were
made to induce the goddess to grant a bountiful
harvest. At night torchlight processions were
arranged, and her worshippers expressed their
sympathy with her at the loss of her daughter,
and assisted in searching for her. The Christian
Festival is fixed for the same date, February 2nd ;
and the ceremonies by day and night identical,
candles being used in place of torches.

III. Festivals of the Saints.

The number of Saints, having their duly
appointed festivals, is very great. Many who
were canonized were martyrs, and their feasts
were kept on the anniversary of their death ;
their entrance into life eternal being considered
of greater importance than their birth into a
world of sin and sorrow. Hence their tombs
became shrines ; and so attractive did they
become, that, by many, life's duties were largely
neglected. The enemies of the Church noticed
this, and charged them with imitating their
pagan ancestors. Virgil, when teaching the
duties of the agriculturist, declares :

"No laws, divine or human can restrain
From necessary works, the labouring swain.
E'en holy days, and feasts permission yield
To float the meadows, or to fence the field,
To fire the brambles, snare the birds, and steep
In wholesome waterfalls, the woolly sheep."[1]

It was intended, by the observance of these days, to stimulate the faith, and inspire with courage those who might be exposed to similar trials. But it was not necessary to adopt customs common in the heathen world. And yet this is what they did. "The classic funeral oblations became Christian; the Silicernum was succeeded by the feast at the Martyr's tomb. Faustus inveighs against the Christians for carrying on the ancient rites. 'Their sacrifices,' he says, 'indeed you have turned into Christian feasts; their idols into martyrs, whom, with like vows you worship; you appease the shades of the dead with wine and meals; you celebrate the Gentiles solemn days with them;—of their life, certainly you have changed nought.'[2]

The saints being so numerous, all that can be

[1] *Georgics* I. p. 361.

[2] Tyler's *Primitive Culture*, II. p. 31.

done is to give a few illustrations, with an account of their originals in heathen Rome.

The Festival of St. John is observed on June 24th, Midsummer Day. As his birth occurred six months earlier than that of Jesus Christ, it was natural that this day should be selected. But from many details of the festival, as it is now observed, it is very evident that it is a continuation of an older one. This was the day on which the sun-god was specially worshipped in old Babylon; it commenced with lamentation at his death, and rejoicing at his resurrection. This was a religious expression of sorrow at the setting and gladness at the rising of this earthly manifestation of the great God. In Babylon the more important ceremonies took place on the Eve of the 24th of June i.e., on the 23rd, and this is the case in the Festival of St. John. The following is an account of the observances in Brittany; in Ireland they are very similar. "Every fête is marked by distinct features peculiar to itself. That of St. John is perhaps the most striking. Towards evening one fire is followed by two, three, then a thousand gleam out from the hill-tops, till the whole country glows under the conflagration. Sometimes a priest

lights the first fire in the marked place, and
sometimes it is lighted by an angel which is
made to descend from the top of a church.   The
young people dance about the fires, for there is
a superstition amongst them, that if they dance
round nine fires before midnight they will be
married in the coming year.   Seats are placed
close to the fire for the dead, whose spirits are
supposed to come there, for the pleasure ot
listening once more to their native songs, and
contemplating the lovely measures of their
youth."[1]   " On that great festival of the Irish
peasantry, St. John's Eve, it is the custom at
sundown to kindle bonfires throughout the
country.   The fire being kindled, a piper plays,
and dancing follows.   When the fire has
burned low, an indispensible part of the
ceremony commence.   Every one of the
peasantry passes through it, and several children
are thrown across it."   It is known that long
before Christianity was introduced into Britain,
the Druids observed a festival on June 23rd.
They made bonfires to please the gods, in order
to secure the ripening of the corn and fruit.   The

[1] *The Two Babylons*, p. 166.

walking through the fire, and throwing children over it, is the harmless survival of the old custom of offering human sacrifices. What possible connection can these ceremonies have with St. John ?

The old Babylonian deity Baal has a place in the Roman Calendar as St. Bacchus, for Baal and Bacchus are different names of the same diety. In the Christian list St. Bacchus is described as a martyr, but his festival is on the same day, which of old was sacred to the Roman god. And under his Greek name Dionysius, another festival is provided for him two days later. This Dionysius became the Patron Saint of Paris, of whom a legend affirms, that, after he was beheaded he walked about with his head under his arm. This strange legend had a very simple origin. It was the custom to represent saints, who had died by the sword, by a headless body. Such was the ignorance and superstition of the people, that an artist's symbol was interpreted as a literal fact. A hymn descriptive of the wonderful walk of St. Denis was usually sung at his festival ; this was omitted for some years, but was restored to the service by order of the Pope.

St. George of England furnishes another illustration of a pagan hero being transformed into a Christian saint. This George rose from a very obscure position, was converted, and became a Bishop of the Church; but owing to his cruelty, was hated and violently put to death, and his body cast into the sea, that no relics might be preserved. The Roman Catholic view of his life is very different. He was born at Cappadocia, entered the army in his youth, was put to death in the persecution of Diocletian, and by his patient endurance of suffering converted the Empress Alexandria with forty thousand men to the Christian faith. In the legend of St. George, two ladies appear to have been enamoured of him. In this and many other details his story is not unlike that of Adonis. Whilst in his encounter with a dragon, there is simply a slighty varying story from what is common in every mythology. It seems as if the story of Perseus had somehow become incorporated with that of St. George. In the heathen story, the conqueror marries the princess he rescued; in the Christian version, a great number of converts are won to the faith.

All Soul's Day is ordained not only to keep

in memory those who have passed away, but, as fitting time for efforts to be made to modify their pains in Purgatory. It was originated by Odils, Abbot of Cluny, at the end of the tenth century, and afterwards adopted by papal authority. "A hermit living near a volcano, where wicked souls were tormented in flames, heard a demon declare that their work of torture was interfered with by the alms and prayers of the faithful, leagued against them to save souls; and especially by the monks of Cluny. The hermit informed the Abbot of what he had heard, in consequence of which Odils decreed, that the 2nd of November, the day following All Saints' Day, should be set apart for service for the departed. He set on foot one of those revivals which have so often given the past a new lease of life. The Western Church took up the practice, and round it there naturally gathered surviving remnants of the primitive rites of banquets for the dead. The accusation against the early Christians, that they appeased the shades of the dead with feasts like the Gentiles, would not be beside the mark now, fifteen hundred years later. All Soul's Day keeps up, within the limits of Christendom, a commemoration of the dead, which combines some touches of pathetic imagination, with relics of savage animism, scarcely to be surpassed in Africa or the South Sea Islands." [1]

On this day friends of the departed lay flowers upon their tombs, priests sprinkle their tombs with holy water, and celebrate masses on their behalf; a practice identical with what was common in pagan times. The visit to the tomb of a loved parent, or child, the decoration of the grave with flowers, as an evidence that they are not forgotten, is a beautiful custom; but the payment for masses as the chief, if not the only way by which their well-being in the spirit world can be secured merits the strongest condemnation. It is opposed alike to revelation and reason. It is a survival of the old heathenism of the Roman Empire; and is in perfect harmony with what is common in heathenism at the present time.

It is sad to see that the ravings of a hysterical monk exert such influence over half of Christendom. How dishonouring is that belief, that human effort is necessary to supple-

[1] Tylor's *Primitive Culture* p. 31.

ment the salvation an infinitely loving Father offers to His sinful children. How it limits the grace of the Lord Jesus Christ, who came as the Saviour, if His work has to be completed by the masses of a priest!

CHAPTER XIV

CELIBACY AND SAINTHOOD

OF the superlative excellence of the unmarried state, the Church of Rome has spoken clearly and fully. In his letter to Timothy, St. Paul wrote: "In the latter times some will depart from the faith, giving heed to seducing spirits, and doctrines of devils;" and as a sign that they had departed from the faith, mentions that they would "forbid marriage." Rome's writers have, in most extravagant terms, commended celibacy, and her rules compel her priests to adopt it. According to her authoritative teaching, the life of man or woman if married, however Christlike and useful, is poor compared with that of those who are buried in a "religious house," and are under a vow not to marry.

The evil commenced in the early days of the Church. Persecution drove some to seek a refuge in the desert; later on, when prosperity came, others sought safety from the seductions of the world, by a life of poverty, seclusion and self-denial. In the thirteenth century, when Dominic and Francis founded the great orders called after them, they simply gave system to what was already a common practice. Many, who submitted to the authority of these great leaders, had already retired from the world; others were attracted to them by the conviction that the monastic life was pre-eminently pleasing to God.

The root idea from which this grew, is the inherent evil of matter, hence it was regarded as the duty of those who wished to live a religious and spiritual life, to get rid of, rather than control their natural appetites and desires. By forsaking the crowded city, and living absolutely alone, or with others of a similar spirit; by spending their time, in fasting, prayer, and watchfulness, it was thought that this could be done. When the great orders were founded, and the Pope's benediction increased their prestige, it became the fashion to join them. Young and enthusiastic people were attracted by the savour of sanctity to enter upon this unnatural life; and those who had drunk deeply of life's varied experience, and had been led to say, "all is vanity," sought a quiet resting place where they could prepare to meet their God.

The connection between sainthood and cebilacy is commonly recognised in the East. In Hinduism its influence is great. The priests however marry. This office is confined to members of one caste, to which there is no entrance, except by birth. Were marriage prohibited to these powerful intercessors with the gods, they would die out. But although marriage is a duty of the priests, as of others, it is considered a specially holy act to leave home and family and assume an ascetic life. These men wander from shrine to shrine, and their blessing is earnestly sought. To add to their sanctity, many of them have destroyed their eyes, arms, or legs, and are pitiable objects. They are said to have gained absolute control over their passions, and hundreds of them may be seen marching quite naked at religious festivals. Their life seems wasted. They are merely parasites on an ignorant and super-stitious people.

In Buddhism there is an almost exact counter-part of what is found in the Roman Catholic community. There is practically no caste in Buddhism. Any one may enter the priesthood, and celibacy is enforced. In addition to the regular priesthood, many enter monasteries and convents, and spend their days in ceremonial acts by which they hope to secure "merit," which can be utilized for themselves or for others.

In the Romish Church there is the regular priesthood, and, in addition, a large army of monks and nuns who have taken a vow to remain unmarried, under the impression that special sanctity attaches to their state. Of these many are actively engaged in tuition, sick visiting, and in the care of the poor and home-less. A great part of their time, however, is devoted to the repetition of prayers, and the performance of purely ceremonial acts. In the "Life of the Religious," St. Alphonsus Liguori eloquently sings the praise of this so-called religious life. "There is no consecration so prefound, so entire, as that of the 'religious,' on the day of their profession, because there is none so purifying, so constant, or so religious. The consecration of bishops and priests is more exalted, as, being a sacrament, it is more noble, conferring a more sublime dignity and ineff-

able character ; yea, it is more powerful, because
it imparts to the mere creature some of the
powers of God. But it is not so complete as
the monastic consecration, because it does not
include a mans entire separation from himself,
and from the world ; it is not so entire, because
it does not absolutely consume the liberty, the
independence, and the spontaneousness of his
nature, it is a great sacrifice and a great sacrament, but not a true holocaust." When speaking
of the evil of unfaithfulness to the vow, he says :
" The violation of the vows is a very grievous sin
against the virtue of religion—the crime of
sacrilege. Man consecrated to God, and to His
service, becomes something divine ; he owes
himself, therefore, religious respect, which re-
bounds even to God ; and if ever he should
dishonour by mortal sin, the vows of poverty,
obedience, and virginity, of which he has made
profession, he would commit an outrage against
the Divine honour, he would be guilty of
sacrilege. What rashness ! What crime ! What
impiety would it not be then to violate your
vows." [1] When this life is so commended, and

Nunnery Life in the Church of England. Appendix.

the forsaking of it so condemned, is it wonderful
that many enter upon it? or, when they have
found the convent-life different from what they
anticipated, that they should shrink from
relinquishing it? In many cases the lack of
food, the constant watching, the monotony of
employment, having proved unbearable, suicide
has put an end to their misery. The pictures of
the "religious" in Christendom and the "saints"
of India greatly resemble each other. But the
Hindu believes in gods who delight in the
sufferings of their servants; the Christian in a
Father who is infinite in mercy and goodness.
Tertullian, writing in the second century,
contrasts the Christians of his day with the
hermits of Indian; had he live a little later, he
would have seen how little they differed. And
he would have seen Christain teachers in public
and private urging young and old to adopt the
ascetic life. "St. Jerome declares, with a thrill
of admiration, that he had seen a monk, who, for
thirty years, had lived on a small portion of
barley bread, and muddy water; another, who
lived in a hole, and never ate more than five figs
for his daily repast; a third, who cut his hair
only on Easter Sunday, who never washed his

clothes, who never changed his tunic till it fell to pieces, who starved himself till his eyes grew dim, and his skin like a pumice stone, and whose merits shown by his austerities, Homer himself would be unable to recount."[1]   A long list of self-inflicted tortures of the "religious" might be drawn out, in which the ingenuity of the sufferers is manifest.   Some ate but little; and that of the poorest kind of food.   Some wore heavy irons on their legs, similar to those at one time ordered for refractory convicts.   Some for the space of forty years never lay down to sleep. Some lived in dens of wild beasts or other uncongenial places.   Some made their homes in the field, eating grass and roots like the animals. Some seldom, others never, washed themselves. St. Simeon Stylites carried this madness in misery to perfection.   He began by being tied to a pillar until the cords cut the flesh, and caused it to putrify.   He ended his career by raising a pillar 60 feet high on which he stood for thirty years, exposed to every change of climate, constantly swaying his body in prayer. And   for   centuries   Bishops   of   the   Church

[1] *History of European Morals*, ii. p. 108.

commended him, and held him up in their impassioned addresses as an example worthy of imitation. This was the state of things for centuries until St. Benedict and others founded orders, in the rules of which a similar spirit is manifest, though the methods are more reasonable.

But it may be said that such doings are not sanctioned to-day. Here is an account of what was seen recently in the Church of the Flagellants in Rome. The whip used was similar to those used in our goals. "The discipline was at night, and was thus arranged. The monks assembled and sat in the choir, where I also sat with them. A few candles only were burning, to enable the brother, who handed round the scourges, to see his way. All the candles except one were then extinguished, and by that feeble light I saw a little, while I heard much of what was going on. The brethren—some of them at any rate, perhaps all—laid aside their garments, and commenced the discipline. The Church resounded with the strokes, but I heard no cries. The monks—thirty or forty—were kneeling opposite each other. The exercise lasted some minutes, and then the lights were

relighted and we departed."[1] Without doubt
this is a modern Christian survival of the old
custom by which the priests of Cybel attracted
the attention and quickened the sympathy of
the worshippers of the deity. The whips of
ancient and modern times are strikingly similar.
And as the monks of the early Christian days
sought to secure their own deliverance from the
power of sin by cruelty on their bodies, the
monks of the later ages seek the same end by
the adoption of similar methods.

Asceticism has ever exerted a powerful
influence over the ignorant and superstitious;
and in some places is as influential as ever.
Bodily discomfort, and self-inflicted pain lead
the masses to imagine that there must be
superior sanctity to compel it; and where there
is superior sanctity, its possessor must have
greater power with God. If men lose sight of
the manifestations of His love in the gift of
His dear Son, they are eager to avail themselves of any help that offers, in order to secure
deliverance from the penalty of sin and the
attainment of other blessings. And the Church

[1] *Rome Pagan and Papal*, p. 44.

of Rome has fostered this error. By making celibacy a condition of entering the priesthood, by encouraging the formation of brotherhoods and sisterhoods, whose members must take the vow to remain unmarried, by praising, in extravagant terms, the piety of those who enter a convent, and urging the young to adopt it, she teaches that such conduct is pleasing God. The same impression is given, when those who are not wholly cut off from their kind, are taught to make their visit to certain Churches as painful as possible. It is no uncommon thing to see people make a circuit round a Church, or repeatedly ascend a flight of steps upon their knees until they bleed. Here pain is inflicted under the impression that it will purchase a spiritual boon. For this, too, there are pagan precedents. Julius Cæsar, it is said, ascended the Capitol on his knees to avert an evil omen; and Claudius is credited with a similar act. Juvenal speaks of a woman seeking to expiate her sin in this manner. " She will break the ice and go into the river in the depth of winter, dip herself three times in the Tiber at early dawn, and then, naked and shivering, crawl on her bleeding knees over the whole extent of the Campus Martius."

In the teaching of Jesus Christ we look in
vain for sanction for such practices. He went
about doing good, and for His disciples prayed,
not that they should be taken out of the world,
but by divine grace kept from evil. There is
not a word in His teaching that can be strained
into countenancing the idea that self inflicted
suffering is a sign of, or conducive to, superlative
holiness. Those who are most like Him are
those who manifest His spirit in the home, in the
family, in the busy mart, in the house of sorrow,
in the social circle, rather than those who hide
themselves in convents, where temptations of a
different kind, though equally deadly, assault
them. The Christian life is a warfare. A life
of seclusion is rather cowardly than commend-
able. It is as though some should hide themselves in a fort, leaving the dangerous and difficult
work to others. Supposing that some who
adopt this life are superlatively good, their light
is hidden ; their lives, if lived openly, might
illumine society, and tend to purify it. The
Saviour's command was, "let your light so
shine before men that they may see your good
works and glorify your Father which is in
heaven."

CHAPTER XV

INSTRUCTING His disciples on the subject of prayer, our Lord said, " Use not vain repetitions as the heathen do, for they think they shall be heard, for their much speaking. Be not ye therefore like unto them." What was the heathen practice which He condemned?

It is an every day sight in India. Many spend hours in repeating the name of a god. There is no real prayer, no asking for favours desired, but a mere repetition of a name. In order to be certain as to the number of times it crosses their lips, a string of seeds, a Rosary is in common use. Sometimes, instead of the mere name of the deity, a doggrel rhyme of sounds without meaning, in which the name occurs is recited. This is termed a mantra, and is taught by the confessor, or guru, at the disciple's initiation. It is supposed to exert magical powers. Whilst its repetition will bring great benefit ; to neglect its use, or to repeat it in the hearing of another person, will bring great suffering. When converted to Christianity some converts are afraid to tell others the mantra they received, lest the forsaken deity should be angry. The rosaries usually have a hundred and eight seeds, as it is a duty to repeat the text as often as this daily. If it is done more frequently, it is a work of merit, or supererogation, and will be credited to him who does it, or can be transferred by him to others.

The common practice of the Roman Catholic Church seems rather to resemble the " vain re-petitions " of the heathen, than prayer as it was taught by the Saviour. One of the commonest acts of penance is the repeated recital of the Lord's prayer, or the salutation given to Mary by the angel ; and special rewards are promised to those who repeat certain holy phrases, or even the name of Jesus Christ. " Pope Sixtus V., in 1587, granted an indulgence of fifty days to Christians as often as they salute others with the words " Praised be Jesus Christ," and as many to him who devoutly answers " Amen." And the same Pope granted twenty-five days

indulgence to those who simply repeat the name
Jesus. Still further he granted plenary indulgence at death, to those who have made a practice
of repeating the name of our Lord, and in their
last hour heartily invoke Him, although they
may be unable audibly to pronounce His name.
And he also promised three hundred days indulgence to those who recite the Litany of Jesus."[1]
These promises were confirmed in 1728 by
Pope Benedict XIII

All are familiar with the phrase common
amongst Roman Catholics of "telling their
beads." The word bead, or as it should be
spelt, bede, in Anglo Saxon, and old English
means a prayer, and then in later times came
to be used for the small perforated balls on a
string used for counting them. A bedesman
was one who was paid to pray for another; and
it was, at one time, a common practice for those
who could afford it thus to pray by proxy. In
the same way in Hindu Society it is a common
practice for a man to lacerate his body, swing
on a lofty bamboo with an iron hook in his flesh,
make a journey on foot a thousand miles to

[1] Butler's *Lives of the Saints*, iv., p. 31.

fetch a vessel of water from the sacred Ganges, and transfer the religious merit of the act to those who were willing to pay for it.

It is uncertain when the use of rosaries became common in the Church; or when the people were encouraged to spend their time in repeating a form of prayer over and over again. In the 4th century it is said that the Abbot Paul was in the habit of repeating the Lord's prayer three hundred times a day, and, to assist him in counting, used pebbles, one of which he dropped into his lap as he finished the prayer. Then came the custom of wearing a necklace which could be used for this purpose. And later on the construction of the more elaborate rosary, which, by its beads of various sizes, can be used for various forms of prayer. The derivation of the term rosary has been traced to various roots. It may come from " The Mystical Rose," one of the many names of the Virgin Mary which occurs in the Litany of Loretta, in commemoration of whom the beads were originally made of rosewood. In the earlier centuries it was the Lord's Prayer that was commonly recited; but as the adoration of the Virgin assumed a more prominent position, the Hail

Mary, largely superseded it. In the rosaries in common use the larger beads are for the Paternosters, the smaller for the Aves.

The "Rosary of the Blessed Virgin" is a litany which is generally known. It is popularly ascribed to St. Dominic, in the twelfth century ; if not arranged by him, it was through his influence that it became popular. It is a series of fifteen exercises, divided into three parts, in each of which mention is made of some event in the life of our Lord, or of the Virgin. This is followed by a Paternoster, Ave, Doxology, and a Prayer. Indulgences are promised to those who voluntarily recite it ; and its repetition is often ordered as an act of penance. The beads of the rosary are used to save the trouble of counting. Virtue seems to lie in the mere mechanical reciting of the words, rather than in the cultivation of a devotional spirit. It is much easier to say, "I have repeated so many prayers," than, "I have truly repented of my sin, and sought divine forgiveness."

The numerous repetitions, even of the Lord's Prayer, seems to be in opposition to the precepts of Jesus Christ. It goes on the assumption common to heathenism, that God, though not

15

spontaneously gracious, may be made so by
human effort or suffering. Jesus condemned
this practice as He said, " Your heavenly Father
knoweth you have need of these things." His
children are commanded to ask for what they
want that their dependence on Him may be
realised; they are forbidden to repeatedly ask,
lest they should imagine that they have to make
an unwilling Father willing to bless.

In securing the " merit " acquired by the mere
repetition of a form of words with least personal
effort, the Buddhists have manifested far more
ingenuity than their Western brethren. They
have invented a praying machine. On a cylinder
the words are engraved, and inside is a coil of
paper on which they are written. By a mere
movement of the hand, the wheel revolves and
the prayer is said a hundred times. The magic
words are printed on flags which the wind wafts
to heaven ; and in many places a large wheel is
kept in motion by running water. By such
mechanical means it is supposed that the Divine
favour can be secured for him who owns the
machinery. Where a prayer, however beautiful
in spirit and expression, is repeated in a purely
formal manner, it is difficult to see in what

respect it is superior in its influence upon the one who offers it, than is the use of his praying machine to the Buddhist.

CHAPTER XVI

CHARMS

THE use of charms has been, and still is almost universal amongst ignorant people. An impression prevails that the powers of the unseen world are inimical to the seen, and can be counteracted by the use of charms. A discoverer of a new one was regarded as a benefactor of the race. Even those who have been taught that a loving Father guards His children have sought protection from evil by their use. "It may be questioned whether this form of fetishism was even more prominent in paganism than in mediæval Christianity."[1] The term "charm" is commonly used for amulets and such things that can be worn upon the body, it is here employed in a wider sense for whatever is supposed to act

[1] *Rise and Influence of Rationalism in Europe,* i. p. 193.

in a magical manner as a protection from evil, and as a means of securing a blessing.

In China it is the universal belief that the air is full of cruel and vindictive beings, many of whom are supposed to be the unhappy spirits of departed relatives. At the gates of the cities, and at the doors of the houses, are images or pictures of deities, whose work it is to keep them away; and, as a bribe to these invisible foes, paper money, clothes, furniture, etc., are burned that the articles represented, may pacify them.

In India charms of various kinds are worn. Some are to protect the wearer from deadly snakes, from various kinds of disease, and in a general way, from harm. Childless wives wear them to secure children; jealous ones to retain a husband's love. Rice from a shrine is put on a child's tongue at the name-giving ceremony to obtain for him a prosperous career; and at death a drop of water from the Ganges, or a grain of consecrated rice is given as a means of cleansing the soul from sin. In Tibet the ashes of specially holy priests are made into medals and worn as charms. In Southern India are many Christians, whose ancestors were won to Christ early in the Christian era. Tradition asserts that St. Thomas

preached the gospel there. To a man they wear
charms similar in shape to those on the neck
and arms of the Hindus. These are images of
the Virgin Mary; those of the Hindus represent
various heathen deities.

In the charms worn by Christians, precisely
similar benefits are expected from their use as
is common in paganism. The following verses
accompanied a charm sent by Pope Urban v. to
his Emperor :—

> " Thunder it chases
>   Sin it effaces,
>   From fire it saves
>   And flood when it raves.
>   Sudden death shuns it,
>   Devils revere it,
>   Enemies fear it.
>   Far from danger are set
>   Both children and mother,
>   Who to make it are met.
>   Where good is found
>   It makes it abound.
>   Big pieces or small
>   Are alike good to all." [1]

Another Pope, Gregory XIV., usually wore an

[1] *Rome, Pagan and Papal*, p. 87.

image of St. Philip Neri, which, he believed had
saved his life during an earthquake at Beneventura. If Popes trusted in charms, it is not
surprising that their people cherished similar
superstitions.

" The sign of the cross was perhaps the earliest
[in use amongst Christians.] It was adopted not
simply as a form of recognition, or as a holy
recollection, or even as a mark of reverence, but
as a weapon of miraculous power; and the
writings of the fathers are crowded with the
prodigies it performed ; and also with the many
types and images that adumbrated its glory.
Thus we are reminded by a writer of the second
century, that the sea could not be traversed
without a mast, which is in the form of a cross.
The earth becomes fertile only when it has been
dug with a spade, which is a cross." [1]

The holy water of the Baptismal font was
supposed to possess the magical effect of changing the spiritual character of those to whom it
was administered, " without any immediate cooperation of deity." In this the Christian's
attitude towards the water, was less rational

[1] *Rise and Influence of Rationalism in Europe*, i., p. 191.

than that of the Hindu towards the Ganges. He
justifies his use of it as a means of soul-cleansing
agency by the assurance that it is a living
goddess, who, by remaining on earth, graciously
provides a way of salvation for the sinner.

The consecrated host is used by many as a
charm. It has been employed as a love charm
by a neglected wife, to render bees fruitful, to
drive away a plague of caterpillars, and as a
cure for blindness. A story is told by Amaliri of
Metz, that when a wicked man was taken to the
grave for burial, the earth refused to receive his
body. St. Benedict gave the friends a wafer,
which was laid upon the corpse, and their
trouble was over.[1]

The cross is very commonly worn as a charm.
It is supposed to be specially effective in driving
away evil spirits. An engraving common in
France represents a child carrying a cross, and
asking his good angel to protect him from a
snake. The angel replies, "Carry that sign
[the cross] before you in confidence, and the
serpent will be powerless."

A few illustrations of the use of charms in the

[1] *Rome Pagan and Papal*, p. 98.

Church will show how common was the faith in their efficacy. In Spain, during the days of chivalry, a knight was not permitted to enter the lists, until he had divested himself of those he commonly wore and made a declaration that he was not secretly protected by them ; to this day, few, if any, of the Spanish troops go into action without one. Bull fighters usually wear them and credit them with their escape ; and it is no unusual thing to find a silver heart of the Virgin, round the necks of Italian banditti."
The Times correspondent in Naples affirms that "the brigands who are taken red-handed in this province are invariably found to have rosaries and relics around their necks." And even when converted to Protestantism, in some cases the old superstitious regard for these things continues. A minister at the bedside of a poor woman noticed that she was fumbling with something under the bedclothes while he was speaking to her. On pressing for an answer as to what she was doing, he discovered that she had some medals as charms, and, with difficulty, was persuaded to give them up.[1] An Indian officer,

[1] *Rome Pagan and Papal*, p. 91.

visiting Rome, called on an honorary chaplain
of the Pope, who was most anxious to win over
his Protestant friend to the true? faith.   Hand-
ing him a medal, he asked him to wear it for
nine days, whilst he and others, prayed for his
conversion.   It is evident that the superstitious
regard for charms is not yet effete; nor is it
confined to those who have enjoyed but few
educational advantages.

In the life of Charles V. is an account of the last
moments of that monarch, which show the
influence of this superstition upon such as he.
" Towards eight o'clock in the evening, Charles
asked if the consecrated tapers were ready.
' The time is come' said he 'bring in the candles
and the crucifix.'   These were cherished relics,
which he had long kept in readiness for the
supreme hour.   The one was a taper from our
Lady's shrine at Montserrat; the other a
crucifix he had taken from the hand of his dead
wife at Toledo.   He received them eagerly from
the Archbishop.   On his bosom was placed the
crucifix, and at the head of the bed, hung a
beautiful picture of our blessed Lady." [1]

[1] *Rome Pagan and Papal*, p. 91.

When the Duke of Monmouth was taken prisoner at Sedgmoor, he was fortified by a charm hanging round his neck; and when the Prince Imperial fell pierced by a Zulu spear, he was wearing a medal of the Virgin. This the Zulus feared to touch. They recognised it as a charm such as they themselves wore, and allowed it to remain on the dead body, lest it should transfer the bad luck of its late owner to the man who might possess it. And to give authority to the use of such things, it is not uncommon to see pictures of the infant Saviour with a charm round his neck, similar to those in use amongst the people. The artists' models probably wore them and so they are represented on the canvas.

As an illustration of the belief in the power of holy water to protect those in danger, the following extract from a letter in a recent journal may be given. The writer was evidently in charge of emigrants. "A storm was raging, when an old woman sent for me. She said she had a bottle of holy water, and that if I sprinkled the ship it might still the storm. I complied with her request; after which she desired me to throw the bottle into the sea, so that it might calm the angry waters."

From what has been said it will be noticed
that the use of charms is not confined to the
more ignorant. Where did Christians learn to
wear them? Certainly not from the Saviour but
from the old paganism. Many in use to-day are
identical in shape and material with those of the
old heathen times; some of them being distinctly
indecent. In other cases the form has been
changed; but the trust in their efficacy remains
the same. "My people have committed two
evils;—they have forsaken me the fountain of
living water, and hewn out broken cisterns which
can hold no water."

The following extract from Virgil will show
that it is from such writings, rather than the New
Testament, that the Church has drawn its
instruction on the use of charms :—

"Charms have the power to draw down the truant
moon from heaven.

Circe, by charms, transformed the trusty band of
Ulyses.

Crushed by the force of charms, the cold snake lies
dead in the meadow." [1]

Amulets, of various materials, were almost

universally worn ; frequently these were images of the gods enclosed in leathern cases. Bells were supposed to be terrifying to evil spirits. Holy water was in common use as a means of purifying the soul, and of protecting from evil, Candles were burned at funerals and other religious services. Emperors wore images of guardian deities, as their Christian successors wore those of guardian saints. In the fields, and at cross roads, images of protecting gods occupied the places where crosses and crucifixes now stand. An image of Pallas, the Palladium of Troy, was supposed to exert such influence that. until it was carried off, the city could not be taken, as the girdle of the Virgin in the Palladium of Tortora in Spain. In the fourth century the clergy were forbidden to sell charms, in the 8th the people were forbidden to wear them ; but the use of them at the present time is almost universal.

THE END.

W. JOLLY AND SONS, PRINTERS, BRIDGE STREET, ABERDEEN.

Printed in the USA
CPSIA information can be obtained
at www.ICGtesting.com
LVHW010200051024
792935LV00002B/294